Church and State

Report of the Archbishops' Commission

Church Information Office, London, SW1

First published 1970

© Central Board of Finance of the Church of England, 1970

Printed in England by
Eyre & Spottiswoode Limited at the Grosvenor Press, Portsmouth

Church and State

Members of the Commission

The Reverend Professor Owen Chadwick (*Chairman*)
The Right Honourable the Earl of March and Kinrara (*Vice-Chairman*)
The Bishop of Chester (the Right Reverend G. A. Ellison)
The Bishop of Leicester (the Right Reverend R. R. Williams)
The Dean of Chester (the Very Reverend G. W. O. Addleshaw)
The Archdeacon of Westminster (the Venerable E. F. Carpenter)
The Archdeacon of Swindon (the Venerable F. S. Temple)
The Reverend Canon W. J. Westwood
The Reverend P. R. Cornwell
D. W. Coe (from 1966–70 MP for Middleton and Prestwich)
The Hon. Mr Justice Cumming-Bruce
Sir Timothy Hoare, Bt
Professor Kathleen Jones
Lady Ogilvie
W. D. Pattinson
Miss Valerie Pitt
W. R. van Straubenzee, MBE, MP (until he became on 24th June 1970
Joint Parliamentary Under-Secretary of State, Department of
Education and Science)

ASSESSORS
Sir John Guillum Scott, TD
D. M. M. Carey
Sir Harold Kent, GCB

SECRETARY
C. P. Hill, CB, CBE

CONTENTS

Preface

Your Graces,

We were appointed to serve under the terms of a resolution passed by the Church Assembly on 10th November 1965, but we were not constituted until almost a year later. The Assembly approved our terms of reference thus: 'to make recommendations as to the modifications in the constitutional relationship between Church and State which are desirable and practicable and in so doing to take account of current and future steps to promote greater unity between the Churches'.

We have held 29 meetings, 16 of them residential. We received evidence from a large number of witnesses, both corporate bodies and individuals. A list of witnesses is given in Appendix F. We thank them.

We have had the help of consultants appointed by the Free Churches and the Roman Catholic Church, who came to one of our residential meetings and gave us written advice and comments, for which we are grateful. Their names are given in Appendix G.

In June 1969 the Archbishops appointed the Earl of March as Vice-Chairman and from 1st October he became acting Chairman.

We regret that we cannot be unanimous in our recommendations. We think, however, that our divisions reflect the various shades of opinion throughout the Church. All of us would welcome some change in the present relationship between Church and State. All of us recognise that if there is to be union between the Church of England and other Churches some changes must be made. All but three of us feel that these changes need not, and indeed should not, lead to formal disestablishment.

All of us are agreed that the Church must have greater freedom to determine its own doctrine and to order its own worship. All of us are agreed that changes in the method of appointing bishops are desirable. We cannot be unanimous, however, about the nature and extent of these changes. Differences exist both about what is desirable and about what is practicable. In the circumstances we have set out in Chapter 3 what seem to us to be two possible alternatives, to which their supporters have appended their signatures.

The main issues are dealt with in Chapters 1, 2 and 3. A number of other matters which naturally arose in the course of our discussion or which were specifically referred to us are dealt with in Chapters 4, 5 and 6.

We regret that three of our number have been unable to sign the Report. Others would not wish to commit themselves to every sentence in it. We hope and believe that what we have written will give the General Synod and the Church the means to decide what is the right relationship between Church and State as the Church moves forward into a new era of Church government.

We owe thanks to our assessors and our secretary and those who have assisted them.

CHAPTER 1

Introduction

The first word that confronted us is the word 'establishment', or the phrase 'The Church of England as by law established'. In this report we have tried to avoid using these expressions. This needs explanation.

We have found the word *establishment* to have more than one sense. It is used in popular language as a way of describing 'those in positions of authority'. Used in this way the word has an overtone of privilege, reaction, apathy and self-satisfaction. We have found it defined as 'the popular belief in a single power élite extending over the political, social and economic life of the nation, current in the late 1950s'.

We have observed that when people (even among our witnesses) attack the Church of England, using the word 'establishment', they sometimes mean establishment in this colloquial sense, and not any particular laws of the British constitution which affect the working of the Church.

This confusion is better avoided.

The word 'establishment' is also used, sometimes, to mean 'the existing system'. We have heard men blame the 'establishment' when they actually complained of the speed of debates in the Church Assembly. No measures that we propose would be likely to affect such processes in the Church Assembly or its successor.

This confusion, too, is better avoided.

It is hard to define what is meant by the term 'Church as by law established'.

The words 'by law established' were originally used to denote the statutory process by which the allegiance of the Church of England to the Sovereign (and not the Pope) and the forms of worship and doctrines of that Church were imposed by law. The phrase distinguished the legality of the national Church from other Churches which were then unlawful and whose worship and doctrines were then proscribed. Today this distinction has disappeared, and the legal implications of the phrase are less obvious.

All Churches have a basis in law. Their constitutions and rules are enforceable under the law relating to voluntary associations. Their property and endowments are held under trusts which are sometimes defined by reference to the doctrines and forms of worship of the

1

Church concerned. Some Churches other than the Church of England have found it necessary to promote legislation to secure or modify their forms of worship or standards of doctrine; e.g. the Church of Scotland Act 1921 and the Methodists Church Union Act 1929. The recent Sharing of Church Buildings Act 1969 was almost as badly needed for the purpose of modifying the trust deeds of the Free Churches as for modifying the laws governing consecrated property of the Church of England.

6 Yet, when all this has been said, the legal situation of the Church of England is different from that of other Churches. The difference lies first in some of the restraints and compulsions of the Reformation statutes, which go beyond or are different in kind from those imposed by the trusts, constitutions and special Acts applicable to other Churches. Secondly, owing to its history, the Church of England has a complex of public laws, mostly statutory, governing its institutions, territorial structure, administration and property, the effect of which is that some changes of quite a minor character require statutory authorisation by Parliament. A note on the historical development of these laws, with a particular account of those most relevant to our purpose, is given in Appendix A to this report.

7 For us 'establishment' means the laws which apply to the Church of England and not to other Churches. The question before us is which of these laws need altering or repealing or relaxing, if the work of the Church is to be executed more effectively in the modern world and if unity with other Churches is to be advanced.

It is important to take the question in this form in order to strip the fact from its surrounding myth. The question is, which of our existing laws give ground for discontent and why.

8 It might have been expected that the principal discontent would be found to be the special relationship with the Sovereign, symbolised in the coronation. For nothing so links the Church, at a superficial glance, with the 'establishment', using that word in the colloquial sense.

We have not found it to be so.

On the contrary, we have found the coronation to be a symbol widely valued, among those who are not members of our Church as well as among those who are.

The representatives of our Church who agreed with representatives of the Methodist Church in framing a scheme for unity, were able to agree in hoping that the Sovereign would continue to have a special place in any united Church.[1]

So far as we can ascertain, the place of the Sovereign, as a symbol of

---

[1]Anglican/Methodist Unity Scheme 1968 p. 98.

national recognition and encouragement, gives rise to very little difficulty, is seldom resented by non-Christians, would not be an obstacle to Christian unity, and is much valued by many persons.

We hope that other Churches will be brought, in a more formal way than hitherto, into the rite of coronation. The rite itself may need further substantial adaptation to meet the times, which we hope to be distant times.

One of the existing relations between Church and State, which is offensive to some, is the obligation of the State schools to provide religious education. The National Society appointed another commission to consider religious education, and so it was not regarded as coming within our terms of reference; and with reason, for historically there has been no legal connexion between religious education and the complex of laws which have been popularly known as 'establishment'. It would be possible for religious education to exist in State schools even if there ceased to be any special relation between Church and State, and possible for religious education to cease while there continued to be that special relation. We have been aware of this problem, but we have not thought ourselves called upon to consider it formally. In this matter all Churches are in the same legal position.

At first sight, then, we have been set the task of considering plans for amendments to the law and constitution of England. We do not doubt that this has been our task. If we could have regarded it as our sole task our work would have been easier and shorter. But for two reasons we have been unable to regard it as our sole task. The first reason lies in the terms of reference which you set us. The second reason lies in our own relation to the society in which we live.

Our terms of reference directed us to listen to, and to respect, the wishes of other Churches. We are the first such Commission on Church and State so to be required.

We have tried, and tried hard, not to identify the interests of Christianity in England exclusively with the interests of the Church of England. We have sought steadily to take a wider view of the question, and to see the Church of England as one important part of the general work of the Christian Churches in England. We have been helped towards this attitude by advice from members of other Churches whom we have been privileged to consult; and by the terms of reference under which we served.

We asked ourselves whether our subject was 'Church and State' only, or whether it was not also 'Church and society'. Previous commissions confined themselves, almost entirely, to the legal constitution of Church and State; and since this was their (and our) brief they might be praised. But we did not see how we could properly answer questions about the legal framework without asking questions beyond the legal framework.

3

For the processes of government are not definable exclusively in terms of the organs of government. The question 'where does power lie?' is well known to result in complex and often surprising answers. In this age attempts to study the nature of the State reflect the shifting balance between legislature, executive, and judiciary, between central and local government, and between all these and a range of other public and semi-public bodies, corporations, tribunals, councils and private interests. Probably this has always been part of the truth in English history; but no age has been so conscious of this truth. Formerly the word 'State' in the phrase 'Church and State' could be limited in terms of Crown and Parliament and statute law. Our age sees that though these are the chief organs of the State, the State is something more subtle, more diverse, and less susceptible of tidy definition.

We therefore tried to look, not only at Church and State, but at Church and society. The limitations on this procedure were evident. If most ordinary Englishmen are polled about Church and State they know nothing about it, do not care about it, and have no complaints about any arrangements that might be found to exist. If the bishops went round asking most Englishmen what to do, and obeyed what they suggested, they would probably end by doing nothing. This would be less because the people admired all that exists than because they were indifferent to what exists and had experienced no reason to grumble. Some of them would hardly know what they were being asked about. An examination of 'society' (supposing that this were feasible) would not necessarily lead to any firm conclusion about ecclesiastical law. But we thought that some results of such an examination might point towards certain conclusions.

13 We therefore needed statistics, and an interpretation of those statistics. We found it easier to get statistics than to get any agreement on what the statistics meant.

14 How many persons in England are members of the Church of England? If we judge by the results of opinion polls, the figure is very high. Somewhere between a half and two-thirds of the population claims membership, which would give a total in the provinces of Canterbury and York of between 23 and 30 million people. This massive adherence is, according to one detailed survey carried out by the Gallup Poll organisation, without bias of sex or age or social class. Official church statistics corroborate this claim, indicating that 66 per cent of the population has received Anglican baptism. Nearly ten million people have been confirmed.

15 Some people have argued the figures do not indicate the reality. They say that men call themselves 'C. of E.' who have no observable religion; brides are married in church because they want ceremony, not Christianity; baptism is a residual custom, still widespread, but increasingly empty of meaning. The figures for Easter communion – a

little over four per cent of the population – give a true picture, it is said, of what is in reality a minority Church.

But (it is said) this is not the worst. These statistics can be shown by the standards of past years to be the statistics of decline. Infant baptisms have fallen from 658 per thousand live births in 1902 to 511 per thousand in 1967. Marriages in an Anglican place of worship have decreased from 64·2 per cent of all marriages in 1904 to 47·4 per cent in 1962. Parochial Easter communicants, 89 per thousand adult population in 1922, dropped to 69 per thousand in 1962, and have since decreased further.

It has been argued that these figures demonstrate a gradual (or a rapid) advance of 'secularisation' in English society. The word is used in two related senses: that religion is declining, in the sense that fewer individuals than formerly practise a religion; and that society is less and less governed by religious considerations in its judgements on politics, literature, economics, law, journalism, and social custom or manners. Society, the argument runs, is becoming a 'secular' society, uninfluenced by religion even in its moral standards; and the ecclesiastical laws which remind the nation of a formerly religious past must sooner or later, probably sooner, be eroded or vanish, less because anyone objects to them than because they have become irrelevant.

However, few of those who are professionally engaged in the social analysis of religion accept a simple or dogmatic reading of the evidence. There is conflicting evidence, and there are conflicting interpretations. Even the simplest statistics which we have quoted here are subject to many qualifications and limitations. The Church of England is not the only organisation to discover a gulf between active and passive members, or to look for ways of involving the nominally-attached more closely in its affairs; and if attendance at church has declined, it can also be observed that many other kinds of public attendance – at political meetings, youth clubs, evening classes, theatres and cinemas – have experienced the same trend. Can we regard frequency of church-going as a straightforward index of religious commitment when audiences of eight or nine million people are reported as watching televised religious services? Does the fact that people go to church less often mean that they pray less often or cease to seek the will of God in their daily lives? Can we continue to base estimates of religious belief or practice on denominational statistics when these leave unrecorded new and more ecumenical forms of worship?

Our examination of source material, both published and unpublished, on the present state of religious belief and practice in England is reported summarily in Appendix D. This illuminated several areas of the problem, and at the same time taught us not to dogmatise on the subject of Church and society. We think it would be premature to expect firm conclusions and confident predictions in what is still a new area of study.

20 In the absence of agreement about the meaning, and even about the nature of the evidence, we have perforce relied on a number of impressionistic judgements. Impressions are private views which may reflect unproven axioms within the mind of the witness. We have never allowed each other to forget that our individual judgements of such impressions are likewise conditioned by hidden assumptions within ourselves; and one of our tasks has been to endeavour to expose these assumptions. We need to advise you on the basis of evidence which we know to be partial, incomplete, and relying on a number of individual opinions, some of which were incompatible with each other.

21 Men have different attitudes in their views of the past. One kind of person is aware of the subconscious associations from the past which thrust themselves into the feelings, judgements, decisions of the present; and believes that no change which fails to face this power in historical continuity is likely to be a change widely accepted. Another kind of person wishes to see things as they are, to strip off the sentiment or the ritual of another age, and to make the Church relevant to the age in which it works even at the cost of demolishing traditions which in the past have elicited affection and loyalty.

22 Some see and value the long tradition and grandeur of English religion. They find a Church of the English people which is as old as the English people and helped to make the English into a people. The Church grew as a 'National Church', that is, not a Church which drew its elect out of a secular society but which aimed to be a 'folk Church', the expression of the spiritual life of the whole of society, permeating its institutions and its many avenues of life. Such minds do not lightly discard the idea of a 'State Church' or a 'National Church'. They see a general, diffused, inarticulate, assent to Christianity, in the body of the nation, by people participating in Christian services at birth, or marriage or death, seeking at times to relate their lives to a frame broader than the frame by which they normally live, not thinking about eternity often but, when they do, reaching out to the Church. They value this heritage. They shrink from any alteration in the ecclesiastical law which might threaten to put it in jeopardy. So far from regretting its existence, they see it as a necessary element in a State where Christian influence has existed for centuries. They are far from thinking it ideal as the practice of a religion, and confess that probably its value and stability is greater in ancient communities and market towns than it is in new housing estates and new towns. They are convinced that nation and Churches would commit an error if they despise this inarticulate feeling by the people that they share in the Christian tradition. It is in this deposit of faith and of goodwill that the great opportunity of the Churches is to be found. They do not

want to see the Church set upon a course to alienate those on the fringe of the worshipping community.

But others suspect that the inheritance of history can be a dead hand, heavy upon the present. They are more impressed by the discontinuities of history than its continuities. Whether or not more people are un-Christian, the statistics do not quite show. But such minds are impressed by the fact that people no longer take the Christian Church for granted, as being something that, because it is there, will always be there. They demand that the Church should justify its existence. The Church must take account of the general questioning of authority and so learn to make its way in the modern world. The organs of mass communication force all historic institutions and attitudes to stand at the bar of society and justify themselves not in terms of past grandeur but of present contribution. Such people often attribute this greater sense of discontinuity to new social facts like technological innovation, urbanisation and a quicker pace of change. They find, or think that they find, more people outspoken in regarding Christianity as fading away; in universities, and in the great cities, and in that artistic and intellectual community which is outside universities. You can find more people (they say) than once you would have found, who perhaps respect some Christians very much, and yet regard Christianity as a survival of a great and vanished age; to be apprehended with affection and sympathy in literature and art, but obsolete for the present purposes of society.

In the face of this outspokenness, some Christians are naturally, and properly, more sensitive to the charge that they survive because they once survived; that they are kept going only by legal or formal inherit-ance from the past. In their task of persuading society that they have something which society needs vitally if it is to survive as a civilised society, they want to be taken as they are, with a gospel and a way of life independent of laws and of ceremony. If they are a minority, they would like to be seen to be a minority, that no man may charge them with professing their faith for the sake of custom, or advantage, or social pressure, or convention.

Such minds, moreover, believe that the Church would benefit from recognising its own predicament. Seeing the relative weakness of the Churches in modern society, they want to lay bare that weakness because they believe that only so will the Church be aware of itself and come to terms with the age in which it lives. They want the Church to be quicker in adjustment, freer in reconstruction, perhaps freer in self-revolution.

The man with a stronger sense of continuity thinks that societies do best when they grow, are adapted, cherish the past while they adjust to the present; and is inclined to claim that this manner of proceeding is characteristic of the English genius. The man with a stronger sense of discontinuity retorts that there are times when a clean break has to be made with the past; a complete turning away from old ways. He suspects that the Church of England has come, or will soon come, to such a time. He does not doubt the power of history, but draws different conclusions from its evidence.

24 In association with these different attitudes to the past, we have found different moods or temperaments. The second type has more sense of urgency, or even agony. Those who think in terms of continuity or adjustment quietly expect a further development. If anyone tells them that the Church is in a crisis they retort that the Church has been observed to be in a crisis every year for centuries. Those who think in terms of reconstruction bear about them an impatience, even a suffering, as though the time of decision slips by while men pretend that all is almost well.

25 We have found several differences in theological attitude.
The differences do not lie in a theology of the State. We have listened to arguments which could be caricatured in these terms: 'the State is evil, keep away from it'. Whatever our differences upon this subject, we are all agreed (with the New Testament and with unbroken Christian tradition) that the State, for all its possibility of evil, is one of God's instruments; that moral laws apply to it; that it has a duty to encourage the good when it can do so expediently, and discourage the bad. Those who say that (in modern circumstances) the State should have nothing to do with the Churches must not be inferred therefore to believe that the State can be, or ought to be, morally neutral. We are all agreed, for example, that the State's duty to education is not derived solely from the material needs of its citizens, and that the State's duty to foster racial harmony is not derived solely from the need to keep the peace. We are all agreed that the State has an interest in the work of the Churches. Whatever else the Churches do or fail to do, they exercise a moral influence; and to any strong moral influence no State can be indifferent.

26 The differences in theology rather concern the nature not of the State but of the Church. They have been difficult to define precisely.
We do not pretend that the following theological attitudes are sharp, nor that they are mutually exclusive, nor that they are an exhaustive catalogue. We do not pretend that anyone holds any of these positions without qualification. But we can discern such attitudes underlying several important areas of disagreement. They affect both our diagnosis of what is and our proposals for what ought to be.

27 Some (including some of our witnesses) prefer to see the Church primarily as the community of faithful and worshipping Christians. Others prefer to see the Church in terms of the community of the baptised if they have not repudiated their baptism and will not set limits to the Church as those who are faithful and practising. Some think that what constitutes the Church is the effective propagation of

the Christian gospel and the pure administration of the sacraments, and are not disturbed by secular interferences in Church affairs if it is directed towards such virtues. Others see the Church as a society coming by succession from the apostles, with its God-given rights of independence and self-government, and regard every intervention from outside as to be deplored and if possible removed. Some think that it is the duty of the Church to seek to transform society and to make it a better society. Others think that it is the duty of the Church to speak to the individual soul to heal and to free, and that if consequences follow for society that is because through the Church those individuals have become true servants of God. Some regard the diffused and inarticulate assent of the English people to Christianity as nothing but opportunity for the Churches; and others, while taking this diffused assent seriously, regard it as a puzzling and ambiguous phenomenon which in some cases is near to Christian faith and in some cases is near to superstition.

Some of these disagreements or differences of theology, which we observe in the Church, have been reflected on the Commission and some of them are fundamental. The curious thing is that with the exception of one main subject we are in large majority agreed in substance on what we ought to aim at. If this is surprising, we remind ourselves that our terms of reference required us to recommend something that would be practicable as well as desirable. To be practicable is to take account of the circumstances. And circumstances have a habit of getting in the way of any rigid application of principles. We have not found that the ideal and the possible are at all points the same. But we have found that we are much nearer to being agreed about the possible than we are agreed about the ideal.

It is to be presumed that you would not have appointed us unless you were aware of discontent with what exists.

We have heard arguments, and witnesses, seeking to persuade us that all is well and nothing needs to be done. They argue in substance as follows:

(1) In the community at large, so far as people are aware of 'Church and State', they are for the most part uninterested and uninformed, and quite content to leave things as they are. So far as that mysterious entity 'the State' has an attitude, it appears to reflect this reasonable contentment with the existing situation.

(2) The comprehensiveness of the Church of England is secured, or at least much assisted, by its historic polity. The legal tradition is a protection for liberal, or evangelical, or anglo-catholic, opinions.

(3) Any prising apart of the links between Church and State could end the national recognition of Christianity.

No one ought to underestimate the force of the opinion here presented.

It happens not to be strongly represented on your Commission. But we must not conceal that some of our witnesses greatly value the ecclesiastical polity of the Church of England and see no particular reason for recommending alterations in what now exists.

30 At the other extreme the National Secular Society offered evidence which proposed a sweeping away of most of the ecclesiastical laws of England. They argued that immigration had brought 'appreciable numbers' of non-Christians to live in England; that the present constitution lent an unfortunate 'credence to the view . . . that England is a Christian country'. They recommended legislation to make the coronation no longer a religious ceremony and not performed by an officer of the Church; to abolish prayers, from whatever quarter, at all official, national, civic and legal ceremonies; to remove the bishops from the House of Lords and to allow Anglican clergymen to be Members of Parliament and to practise at the bar; to abolish the statutory position of the church courts so that they may become simply internal disciplinary bodies; to abolish the right of Parliament to control the worship of the Church; and to remove the endowments of the Church of England.

31 Your Commission is not naturally in sympathy with all these suggestions. And yet the reason for alteration is one which we cannot quite reject; for it is the reason of abstract justice.

Those who dislike Christianity naturally dislike laws which make it appear as if England is a Christian country.

It is not our opinion that England wants to appear non-Christian. But we cannot dismiss this question of abstract justice out of hand. Some of our laws descend from a time when Church and State were identical, when the Church was believed to be society in its religious aspect, and when to call the Church of England the 'national' Church meant that it was the Church of the nation. We used to doubt whether any of our laws today would suggest this to anyone. But we have been surprised to find that they do; that some suppose the Church of England to claim, not only to be the Church of its members, but to be the Church of all Englishmen; and that some imagine us never to have reconciled ourselves to the Toleration Act, the emancipation of Roman Catholics, the freeing of Nonconformists and later Jews from their civil disabilities, or the admission of atheists to Parliament.

We want to make it clear (while we blush to assert something so obvious) that we are not blind to the plural nature of English society. The Church of England is one Church among several. So far as it is called a 'national' Church, it professes a mission to all the nation. It does not claim to cast its shadow over men or women who repudiate it. The Church of England does not suppose that it is an 'expression of society', 'the religious aspect of society'.

We had supposed that these were platitudes. We have found that (with some) they are not.

And if they are not, there is an argument in abstract justice for amending some ancient laws which hint at an 'identification' between the Church and a society containing many persons who do not profess to be Christian.

This is a reason for wanting Church and State to stand further apart. We doubt whether this reason will weigh heavily in the future argument. Englishmen do not willingly wind themselves up to the abstract. But it has lain under some of the discussion, and it cannot be neglected.

Of course the Church of England is committed, by its history, its name, and its heritage, to a national mission. No amendment of the laws could alter the vocation to a national mission; and if a national mission, then a comprehensive attitude to Christian opinions, and no desire to draw narrow lines to distinguish the godly from the ungodly, and a reluctance to accept a move towards sectarianism.

Apart from this abstract question, the force of which is not easy to determine, three main reasons prompt us to recommend changes. They are practical reasons: (1) the needs of the movement towards reunion; (2) the needs of the pastoral mission of the Church; (3) the constitutional development of the Church.

(1) *The needs of the movement towards reunion*

You have included in our terms of reference a directive that we must bear in mind the possibilities of Christian unity. That means in practice that you required us to take account of the opinions of Free Churchmen and Roman Catholics. Free Churchmen and Roman Catholics, though not agreed on whether it is good for a Church to have links with a State – for some of the Free Churchmen whom we heard were in favour of an 'establishment' provided that it was reformed – are all agreed on wishing those links to be modified. And if union were to take place with any denomination (especially the possibility that lies not so remotely, a union with the Methodists at stage 2 of the unity scheme) that union could hardly take place without substantial modification of the legal situation of the Church of England.

In parish and town life the Churches of today want to act together, and so far as the community is concerned, are expected to do so, whether in providing opportunities for worship on special occasions in the life of the community, or in action or comment on matters of public and social concern. This co-operation at all levels of Christian work, which runs from education and broadcasting at the national level, to the local council of Churches, is one of the most promising features of the life of the Churches in our day. And it has suggested a reason why it would be proper for the nation, as well as the Church of England, to take account of the views of Free Churchmen and Roman Catholics about the laws of the Church of England; even if no immediate prospects of Christian unity, in a more organic sense, could be offered.

11

It may be a matter of argument whether England is growing more secular. What looks probable is that England is growing less denominational. The fights of ancient days can still produce placards outside Lambeth Palace, or an occasional interrupter at a sermon. But the nation as a whole smiles at the fanatic and is unmoved. Young people are impatient with the obstacles inherited from history. The distinction between Anglican and Methodist is real enough; and yet it has come to seem, whether to Anglicans or Methodists or those outside either church, less meaningful than formerly; and what is true of those denominations, with their close ties of sympathy in origin and history, appears to be true among the denominations at large.

36 In England (according to opinion surveys) there are about six million who profess to be Free Churchmen, four and a quarter million who profess to be Roman Catholic. Over 70 per cent of the country claims to be Christian, and on top of that are the two and a quarter million adherents of other faiths including the Jewish community.

37 Over the last decades the State has reflected this feeling among the people. The reality of the moment is that while the Church of England has a unique polity in its connexion with the State, it is the Churches generally which the State recognises. In education, hospitals, prisons, the armed services, it has sought to provide opportunities for all the leading denominations. Radio and television have provided for the sharing of religious broadcasting amongst the main religious groups. The Crown has appointed leading members of other denominations to the House of Lords, who speak there besides the bishops of the Church of England. The State also listens to those who repudiate all Churches. But it rightly listens to the Churches because they represent a big influence in English society, because Christianity is the dominant religious influence, because there is so widespread an acceptance of Christian values and Christian standards.

So far as what we recommend might help towards Christian unity we are confident that the State would place no obstacles in the way.

38 (2) *The needs of the pastoral mission of the Church*
In times of rapid change the Church needs to take radical steps in deploying men or buildings or money, in providing for new forms of service, in welcoming the links with other denominations and making those links stronger, and in a variety of practical ways which require a tiresome expenditure of energy over detail but which issue at last in the better provision of word and sacrament.

A few experts in these matters believe that these adjustments would be easier if the Church of England severed all links with Parliament. For reasons which we give later (when we consider the relation between Church and Parliament) we are persuaded that though in some respects this is true, in other respects it is not true; though we are far from suggesting, as will be seen, that there ought to be no modification of the present relationship between Church and Parliament.

We have heard several witnesses argue that the pastoral mission of the Church will be made easier if the links with the State are fewer. The arguments have taken various forms:

(a) Some people are in revolt against established institutions and structures. Even to be called 'established' projects an unfortunate image of an institution. The links with the State associate the Church with a bourgeois system and power structure which is being sharply criticised. At a time when all governments are under question, it is better for the Churches to keep far away from government.

(b) The Church of today needs to be seen as a servant Church, not a ruling Church. Confessedly the Church is a servant Church and not a ruling Church. But it needs not only to be so but to be seen to be so. Its old links with the State hint at privilege; at power which comes not by the influence of charity but by the inheritance of an ancient secular superiority.

(c) The moral witness of the Church is weakened if it has links with the State. It cannot protest so vigorously against the State's action where the State is believed to be acting immorally.

We have listened to these differing arguments with respect. We are sharply disagreed on how much weight to attribute to them. Those, for example, who do not accept the argument (c) above (that the moral witness of the Church in protesting against government may be weakened by historical links with government) hold that men like William Temple or George Bell could not have been so influential in their utterances unless they had been granted a secure place within the State from which they could speak to the authorities of the State. They find it difficult to base any practical conclusion on this argument for which in the nature of the case no reliable evidence can be produced.

But although we are not agreed on these arguments, and hold with them or against them, sometimes strongly, we find ourselves in a situation where we cannot quite dismiss the pastoral argument.

We are told, in effect, that some people will not accept the pastoral endeavour of the Church of England because they associate it with 'establishment' in the colloquial sense; that is with 'them'. And this fear of 'them' is said to be derived from, or to rest partly upon, the historical links with the State evident in some of the laws of our ecclesiastical polity.

As a Commission we are not prepared to make this argument our own corporately. It is impressionistic, its force will vary from man to man, from region to region, from social group to social group. But after long and anxious reflection on this matter, we have felt it right to set down the argument as one which is exerting influence.

13

42 We mentioned earlier that if men consulted the opinion of the majority they would probably end by doing nothing, because the majority of Englishmen (so far as can be judged) seem to be content with what is.

We must now mention that some members of our Church are not in the least content. A body of members of the Church of England – not, we guess, a majority of the practising members, but a substantial body, certainly of sufficient weight to be taken very seriously – dislike, and in some cases detest, more than one aspect of the existing relations between Church and State. Even if they should prove numerically to be a minority of the practising members we are confident that they are neither small in numbers, nor fanatical, nor eccentric in opinion; but that the group contains many sensible men who have at heart only the effective work of the Church of England, and the effective witness of Christianity, in this country.

43 (3) *The constitutional development of the organisation of the Church of England*

As the State became impartial in religion, the Church of England naturally developed its structure of self-government. It became more and more autonomous.

1852 The Convocation of Canterbury resumed debate.

1861 The Convocation of York resumed debate.

1866 First diocesan conference.

1885 House of Laity attached to the Canterbury Convocation.

1892 House of Laity attached to the York Convocation.

1870–1903 Development of parochial church councils.

1904 First meeting of Representative Church Council, combining both Convocations and House of Laity.

1919 Representative Church Council is turned into National Assembly of Church of England (Church Assembly) and given the right to pass Measures which with the assent of Parliament have statutory force. Parochial church councils made compulsory.

1947 Process of revising the Canons, substantially complete 1967.

1963 Ecclesiastical Jurisdiction Measure removes the Judicial Committee of the Privy Council as the highest court of appeal and substitutes a court of appeal in cases of doctrine and ritual devised by the Church Assembly.

1965 Alternative and Other Services Measure permits Convocations and House of Laity to sanction (for an experimental period, see below) new forms of service.

1969 Synodical Government Measure reconstructs representative system in parishes, rural deaneries, and dioceses, and associates House of Laity with Convocations in all the work of the Church, including doctrine and liturgy.

The Commission does not believe in 'historical necessity', or think that because history has gone in one direction for some time it will necessarily continue for ever to go in the same direction. But here over 120 years appears a steady movement towards autonomy; the decline of state intervention; in some parts of the constitution the vanishing of state intervention; the steady construction of a representative system of government. It is not a wild prediction that (unless the constitution of Britain were shattered out of its steady development by some cataclysm) the trend will continue, until the Church of England is autonomous and the intervention of the State will vanish, except so far as States must always be prepared to ensure that every Church is faithful to the trusts by which it is a corporate entity.

To say that history moves in a certain direction is not a valid argument for helping it to move in that direction unless one is confident that the direction is beneficial. But it will be evident to everyone that the more representative the system, the more knobbly appear those surviving parts of the old constitution which do not fit the representative system: such as, for example, private patronage, or parliamentary veto upon the Prayer Book. We do not assert that a totally representative system would be an ideal constitution. All constitutions need their logic modifying if they are to work. But the seventies will be a time (we think it fairly safe to predict) when the representative system, built up slowly since 1852, will more fully establish itself as the proper organ to which members of the Church of England look when they wish to be represented in matters concerning the Church, and if that happens (we believe that we already see it happening) the marriage between the ancient constitution and the new representative system will bring unusual discomforts, and probably dangers, if the laws of our ecclesiastical polity remain in other respects precisely as they are.

For example: in 1927 and in 1928 the Church Assembly passed a Measure for a new Prayer Book. In each year the House of Lords accepted it and the House of Commons rejected it. This caused much discussion, some anxiety, and a measure of ill feeling. But it was not a calamity for the Church of England. It was not a calamity for the Church of England amongst other reasons because many members of the Church of England regarded themselves as better represented in religious matters by the House of Commons than by the Church Assembly. But forty years later the same loyalties are not so evident. The Church Assembly has developed its own loyalties and has been turned into the General Synod; the House of Commons has withdrawn a little more from church matters, as recent Measures and recent debates on Measures show. And if under these new conditions a General Synod, which commanded the loyalty of many practising Anglicans, proposed a new Prayer Book, and a House of Commons, which was no longer seen by many practising Anglicans as its representative in church matters, were to veto it, it is possible to predict a constitutional crisis and perhaps a calamity for the Church of England resembling that which happened, in not too dissimilar circumstances, to the Church of Scotland in 1843.

Some may accuse us of crystal-gazing about the future. We do not ask them to take much notice of soliloquies on historical trends, or of misty prophecies. But they will take the point if we put it like this: there is a rub between the ancient historical polity and the new representative system. This rub may increase rather than diminish. In our judgement the only way to prevent it from increasing, is to jettison, at least, one or two features of the ancient historical polity which would be likely to be ever more obtrusive as the representative system develops under its inherent constitutional momentum.

CHAPTER 2

The Relation with Parliament

In whatever direction we have turned – to some members of the Church of England, to representatives of the Anglican communion, and representatives of the Free Churches and the Roman Catholics – we have found two sources of disquiet:

(i) the veto which Parliament exercises, or could exercise, over forms of worship in the Church of England;

(ii) the manner in which the bishops of the Church of England are appointed.

In the light of our terms of reference which compel us to take into account the views of other Churches, we have found that both these sources of disquiet run sufficiently deep to have a weighty effect on relations between our Church and other Churches.

In this chapter we deal with the first of these sources of disquiet.

THE MEANING OF PARLIAMENTARY VETO

Parliament has power in this, as in all fields, to pass Acts prescribing what is to be done or not to be done, and to provide for their enforcement. But in practice Parliament's power is a negative one, i.e. to veto changes proposed by the Church which require statutory authority, and this power derives from the following circumstances.

The permanent worship of the Church of England is contained in the Book of Common Prayer of 1662 which is enforced by the Act of Uniformity 1662 and the Clerical Subscription Act 1865, together with other forms of service authorised by the Act of Uniformity Amendment Act 1872. Until 1965 no other forms of worship could lawfully be used without authorisation by Act of Parliament or Church Assembly Measure. As already mentioned, in 1927 and 1928 Parliament refused to approve Measures authorising the use of a new Prayer Book, which would have been alternative to the Prayer Book of 1662. Thus it used its negative power, forty years ago, to prevent the Church of England from modifying its forms of prayer.

In 1965, by approving the Prayer Book (Alternative and Other Services) Measure of that year, Parliament granted temporary powers to the due authorities of the Church to approve new forms of service, of an experimental character and alternative to the Prayer Book of 1662. These powers will effectively expire in 1980. We understand

17

that it was the expectation of those who framed the Measure that, at the end of the experimental period, the Church would return to Parliament with a new Measure authorising another Prayer Book, either in place of or alternative to the Prayer Book of 1662, which Parliament would then be asked to approve. Once again, as in 1927 and 1928, the Church's proposals for liturgical reform would be debated on the floor of the House of Commons and might again be rejected. Even if the Measure were passed, the Church would not gain freedom over its worship, because any future changes would again be subject to the parliamentary veto.

Here lies the first big source of disquiet.

51 This constitutional situation has its defenders. We have found it defended in the pages of *Hansard*. It has been defended on your Commission. The defence may be stated in two ways:

(i) Some people belong to the Church of England more because they are English than because they are Anglicans. This 'national' aspect of the membership of the Church of England, vague and inarticulate though it is, is better represented by Parliament than by the Convocations or the Church Assembly, which represent the clergy and the more church-conscious kind of laity. It is argued that we should shrink from entrusting control over the worship of the Church of England to a body like a General Synod, where ecclesiastical interests, though not exclusive, would necessarily be more prominent; that the effect would be likely to be a narrowing of viewpoint.

In this way it has been argued that the House of Commons is the lay representative of the Church of England; a better lay representative, at least, than the lay representatives in Church Assembly or General Synod.

(ii) The Church of England is in one of its aspects a kind of trust, or rather aggregate of trusts. It has the duty of teaching people certain things and in a certain way, and holds endowments (like any other trust) on this condition. Persons have bequeathed money on the assumption that it will not be in substance other than it is. Parliament can act as an impartial tribunal to protect the rights of citizens to worship in accordance with the traditional liturgy of the Church of England and the rights of those who have endowed churches for the purpose of such worship.

52 We have carefully considered these two arguments for the existing state of affairs. We respect them, and yet find them unrealistic.

53 First, the situation does not work. Parliament can refuse to sanction liturgies but cannot prevent them being used. It refused to sanction the 1928 Prayer Book and large parts of the 1928 Prayer Book came into common use. For they were necessary to pastoral work, and were universally agreed to be both Christian and loyally Anglican.

Secondly in recent times Members of Parliament have criticised the constitution which forces them to debate matters that do not seem to concern them. In 1964, for example, a Measure concerning the vestures which the minister should wear when officiating in church came before Parliament for final approval. Many Members of Parliament, if we may judge from *Hansard*, found it not only odd but wrong that they should be debating such a Measure. Mr Lubbock formally asked the Prime Minister (23rd July 1964) if he would think of some means of divesting the House of Commons of responsibility for Measures of this kind. On 30th July 1964 Mr Chuter Ede, in a moving speech before his retirement, regretted the constitution which permitted non-Anglicans to discuss and vote on such Measures. One of the speakers in the debate confessed to 'a feeling of almost indecent embarrassment', and continued (*Hansard*, Vol. 699, p. 1910): 'That serves to underline the implicit plea which many have made tonight, that the sooner the Church of England can be perfectly free to discuss these important matters and to decide them for itself, the better it will be for the Church and ourselves'.

Not only the record of debates but also our private inquiries show that many Members of Parliament feel something unfitting in the present constitutional situation over Measures concerning worship. We do not assert that all Members of Parliament wish to divest themselves of this responsibility. It is clear from the record in *Hansard* that a very few members are afraid that, if Parliament so divests itself, the Church of England might move towards Rome, or might move in an opposite direction to that of Rome, in short that the Church of England might cease to be itself, if it were given the right to decide its modes of worship. As we observe the Church of England, we think these fears alarmist, and the approval of important recent Measures has shown that they no longer carry weight in Parliament as a whole.

On the Prayer Book (Alternative and Other Services) Measure 1965 there was no division in either House of Parliament, which is a striking fact. And when the Archbishop of Canterbury first brought forward the motion for approval, he considered the question of what would happen at the end of the period and said: 'Perhaps by that time Church and State may together have discovered some new means of legislating for future needs' (*Hansard*, Vol. 263, p. 655). It may be noted that the later sections of the Measure gave permanent powers to the Convocations and bishops to approve and use services on occasions not provided for in the Book of Common Prayer, and thus Parliament conceded to the Church some permanent independent authority over forms of worship. Two years earlier, by approving the Ecclesiastical Jurisdiction Measure 1963, Parliament accepted the view of the Church authorities that the final court of appeal in questions of doctrine and worship should be changed from the Judicial Committee of the Privy Council, to which some churchmen objected as a State court, to a new final court decided on by the Church authorities which would comprise among its members bishops sitting in the House of Lords and would be assisted by bishops and theologians appointed by the Convocations. Since 1965, in connection with the revision of the Canon Law, several Measures have been passed amending the rubrics in the Prayer Book relating to Holy Communion, ordination and baptism, without any serious degree of opposition. Parliament accepted without demur the proposals for synodical government contained in the Synodical Government Measure 1969; and this will have the inevitable effect of encouraging the trend towards independent action.

57 We believe, therefore, that we have received a sufficient invitation, part implicit and part explicit, from Members of Parliament individually, as well as from Parliament acting collectively, to seek some further scheme for the control of worship by the Church, which might be acceptable to both Church and State.

58 Thirdly, many members of the Church do not like the existing constitutional position over control of worship. Our predecessors of 1935, and our predecessors of 1952, both declared that the present position was 'indefensible'. We have not found this feeling to have diminished but rather the contrary. For we have found an enormous sense of relief (we think we are not overstating it) at the passing of the Prayer Book (Alternative and Other Services) Measure of 1965, whereby (in effect) the Convocations and the House of Laity (now the General Synod) were given control over worship for 14 years.

59 We cannot think that either Church or Parliament could countenance a return to the situation which prevailed before 1965.

60 We are as far as possible from wishing to blame the House of Commons for the constitution of the past. That House has acted with a steady consideration and courtesy towards the Church of England as to other Churches. But we agree with those Members of Parliament who have expressed the view that the present constitutional situation is in need of amendment.

61 It is natural that many Free Churchmen object to the parliamentary veto. Members of the Church of Scotland and of several non-Anglican bodies in England have testified that they find a parliamentary veto over the worship of the Church of England to be 'intolerable'. Some witnesses are inclined to exaggerate the extent to which Parliament in the twentieth century has influenced or can influence the worship of the Church of England. But even when allowance is made for such exaggeration, there is no doubt that, being Free Churchmen, they object strongly and on principle to the constitutional situation. The Church must be free, they say, to order its worship. They do not see

the House of Commons as in any sense the lay representative of the Church of England. Nor do they see Parliament as an impartial tribunal deciding whether an innovation is compatible with the essential character of the Church of England. They regard it as an erastian system which should be ended, both for the sake of Parliament and for the sake of the Church.

Between the representatives of other denominations which gave evidence to us we naturally found some differences of attitude. They were, however, all agreed that they could not unite with a Church which had the particular relation to the State which the Church of England has, whereby Parliament has a veto on the forms of service used. The 1963 and 1968 reports on Anglican-Methodist unity both approved the following: 'It is to be assumed that the united Church will be free to settle its own forms of doctrine, worship and discipline . . . with the same freedom from State control as is now possessed by the Church of Scotland'.

We do not think that the opinions of the Free Churches alone should sway this question unless other considerations entered into it. The Free Churches have always wished to stand further away from the State. Moreover, it is not sensible for the Church of England to seek changes in its relation with the State only for the sake of a future union, still a hypothesis, with another Church; a unity which on quite other grounds might fail to be consummated. But you gave us terms of reference which require us to take future moves towards unity into consideration. And there are good reasons, as we have shown, both from the point of view of Parliament and the Church of England, why the Church should move in the direction of greater freedom to order its worship. It is right then to give due weight to the opinions of Free Churches that such a movement is necessary to the cause of unity.

A similar degree of weight may be given to one other responsible body of opinion, which sought to persuade us to recommend that the Church should move in this direction; representatives from some of the Anglican Churches overseas. On the occasion of the Lambeth Conference of 1968 we were able to consult four of the primates or archbishops from the Anglican Communion. They did not take identical views of the English situation, but they were unanimous that from the point of view of the Anglican Churches overseas the existing parliamentary veto upon changes in the Prayer Book of the Church of England was felt to be something unfitting in the Church from which their Churches sprung; and that their own experience of freedom in ordering their own worship ought to remove any fears in England that a further transfer of authority from Parliament might lead to undesirable consequences.

65 Mention has already been made of such fears felt by a few Members of Parliament. Similar attitudes and views have been forcibly put to us by certain of our witnesses and are represented on your Commission. They cannot be precisely defined, but some attempt must be made to describe them in general terms.

66 It is felt or suspected that the veto checks 'clericalism'; and that if it did not exist, bishops and clergymen would vote together in the assemblies of the Church, and would influence an allegedly complaisant laity to vote with them, and might thus succeed in narrowing the doctrine of the Church, or in making it less 'national', less comprehensive, less tolerant. As to this, we think that the laity, as they have hitherto been chosen by parishes and diocesan conferences, are much less complaisant that is sometimes alleged. The most 'clerical' age of English Church history since the Reformation – not in the sense of wrongful professionalism on the part of the clergy, but in the sense that the voice of laymen was least effective in the Church – was the age between 1874, when Parliament finally ceased attempts to govern the Church directly, and 1919 when Parliament gave a measure of legislative authority to a Church Assembly which included a House of Laity with its own veto. We believe that the influence of the laymen will be increased and not diminished if the Church of England is entrusted with authority to determine finally its own forms of worship and liturgy.

67 The new Synodical Government Measure has transferred most of the powers of the Convocations of Canterbury and York, which have no lay representation, to a new General Synod, the constitution of which is based on that of the Church Assembly and contains a House of Laity with a power of veto. This House represents, as did the Assembly, a broadly based parochial electorate, the normal qualifications for which are baptism and residence in the parish. The new Measure provides for setting up more effective diocesan synods, in place of the present unwieldy diocesan conferences, and also more effective deanery synods which will be able to provide a channel of communication between the parishes and the higher bodies. All this strengthens the voice of the laity.

68 Apart from the vague fear of 'clericalism', we have found a fear that, if the parliamentary veto were removed, the organs of the Church might seek to depart from the standards of doctrine which are fundamental to the Church of England; that, for example, the sovereignty of the Bible might be tampered with, or the doctrine of justification by faith abandoned, or the true doctrine of the sacraments excluded from the formularies. It is feared that a freedom to experiment in worship might lead to the teaching or implying of doctrines which are not those

of the Church of England. Here we believe that the rights of the bishops and clergy secured in the constitution of the new General Synod, and still entrenched in the provincial Convocations which are to retain some reserve powers in this field, together with the powers of the House of Laity of the General Synod possessing a veto in all matters, will be more effective in preventing 'aberrations' than any parliamentary veto could be. We do not see how Parliament could recognise an 'aberration', i.e. could properly decide whether a change in liturgy or in the formulation of doctrine amounted to a fundamental change in the character of the Church. As we have said, Members of Parliament themselves believe that they are ill-fitted to perform the task of an impartial tribunal in this sphere.

We therefore recommend that a Measure be prepared to ensure that the authority to order forms of worship, already granted in part and for a time by Parliament to the Convocations and House of Laity, should be granted finally to the General Synod; under safeguards to be mentioned hereafter.

SAFEGUARDS

The temporary powers granted by the Prayer Book Measure of 1965 are subject to three limitations or safeguards:

(a) The new forms of service cannot supplant the services in the Book of Common Prayer. The latter remain lawful and available and no new form of service can be used in any parish without the agreement of the parochial church council.

(b) The new forms of service must in the opinion of the Convocations (in future the General Synod) be 'neither contrary to, nor indicative of any departure from, the doctrine of the Church of England'.

(c) The new forms of service must be approved by a two-thirds majority in each House of each Convocation and agreed by a two-thirds majority of the House of Laity of the Church Assembly. Under the Synodical Government Measure the powers are exercisable by the General Synod, and each of the three Houses of Bishops, Clergy and Laity will have to approve the services by a two-thirds majority.

The question arises whether in the future these safeguards are necessary. They will limit the freedom of action in the General Synod. One of the crying pastoral needs of our time is the need to adjust or create forms of worship so as to make them more meaningful to persons not brought up within the mellow tradition of Anglican devotion. This pastoral concern is bound to mean a desire that the period of experiment shall continue, and it is a main reason why neither Church nor State could countenance a return to the constitutional situation which prevailed before 1965.

72 During this period of experiment we have no doubt that the Book of 1662 ought to remain available to those parishes that wish to use it, and that its availability will thus continue for very many years. The difficult question is whether its permanent availability should be ensured by incorporating the first safeguard in the new Measure which is to give permanent powers to the General Synod, so that the Book of 1662 could then only be amended or discontinued by recourse to a Measure in Parliament.

73 As a Commission we take two views of this question.

(1) Some of us think that the General Synod should in the last resort have the power to authorise a new Prayer Book which would supersede the Book of Common Prayer 1662. We yield to no one in our love of the 1662 Book and in our recognition of its place in the life of the Church of England. We would deprecate any suggestion that our proposals constitute a recommendation that the Book of Common Prayer should be forthwith abolished. We are confident that the use of the 1662 Book will continue to be authorised in the foreseeable future and that it would be a permitted alternative so long as it was wanted. But we hold it as a matter of principle that the General Synod should ultimately be the arbiter of the services which are authorised in the Church of England.

(a) Those who hold this view believe that the idea of uniformity is one which the Church of England should not lightly jettison. There will, so far as we can foresee, always be the need for some Book of Common Prayer. After the period of experiment it will be necessary to decide what services shall and what services shall not be incorporated in the Prayer Book. We think that the General Synod should have the power to decide upon the contents of that book.

(b) The safeguard of a two-thirds majority in each of the three Houses of the General Synod will be ample protection against any ill-considered desire to prevent the use of services which are still valued by worshippers. We are confident that the General Synod could be trusted to use the power to produce a new Prayer Book, if this should prove necessary, wisely, charitably and with a full understanding of the needs of the Church.

(c) If there is built into the Measure which we propose a perpetual right for any congregation to use the Book of Common Prayer 1662 the consequence would be that the Church of England could never secure a new Prayer Book without recourse to Parliament. We are all agreed that the control of worship should pass from Parliament to the General Synod. We think it undesirable therefore to leave with Parliament this residual veto upon the control by the Church of its worship.

(2) Others of us take a different view. We think it necessary to build into the enabling Measure the safeguard that any congregation

which so wishes shall have the right to use the 1662 Book.

(*a*) We believe that a proposal that the General Synod should have power to abolish the use of the Book of Common Prayer 1662 would be unacceptable to the Church at large, to Parliament, and possibly to the General Synod. The 1662 Book is a noble heritage of England and the Church of England comparable to the Authorised Version of the Bible, and any suggestion, however ill-founded, that it might be superseded would arouse as strong feelings as would talk of prohibiting the reading of the Authorised Version.

(*b*) We do not accept that the Church of England ought ever to contemplate a return to so restricted a concept of uniformity as is suggested above.

(*c*) We think it paradoxical to preserve the Book of Common Prayer as one of the fundamental standards of doctrine in the Church of England and yet to provide for its possible prohibition for worship by the General Synod.

(*d*) We do not agree with the view that Parliament would be left with an improper veto upon the worship of the Church, for no one suggests that Parliament should be able to insist that a congregation not willing to do so should be compelled to use the 1662 Prayer Book.

(*e*) What we wish to do is to preserve the liberty of the individual congregation to use this historic rite along with other rites which may be authorised.

The Commission is divided on this issue. It would be possible to draft a Measure recommending that this safeguard should be preserved, and that congregations should still have the right to use the Book of Common Prayer 1662; or to draft a Measure recommending that it should not be preserved. The decision must be left to the General Synod.[1]

Whether or not the right of congregations permanently to use the Prayer Book is or is not incorporated, the Prayer Book of 1662 would not lose its authority as one of the fundamental formularies for the teaching of the Church of England. As further new forms of worship are authorised they must not contradict the teaching of the Prayer Book and Ordinal of 1662. This brings us to the second safeguard set out in paragraph 70 above, which we are agreed should be incorporated in the new Measure.

We are also agreed that the third safeguard of a two-thirds majority in each of the three Houses of the General Synod is desirable, both in

---

[1]See Appendix B.

itself, and as a reassurance to those who fear rapid change. This would be additional to the safeguard contained in Article 7 of the Constitution of the General Synod under which all provisions 'touching doctrinal formulae or the services or ceremonies of the Church of England', may be referred for the separate consideration of the provincial Convocations and the House of Laity and may be vetoed by single Houses of either Convocation or by the House of Laity.

77 *Our recommendations on the safeguards (paragraph 70) are as follows:*

    (*a*) *During the long period in which the Book of Common Prayer is available, the choice between it and any new services should lie with the parish. The General Synod needs to consider whether or not the permanent availability of the Prayer Book should be included in the draft Measure on the ordering of worship;*

    (*b*) *new forms of worship must not contradict the teaching of the Prayer Book and Ordinal of 1662;*

    (*c*) *no change should be made unless approved by a two-thirds majority in each of the three Houses of the General Synod.*

FORM OF NEW MEASURE

78 The present temporary powers under the Prayer Book (Alternative and Other Services) Measure 1965 have their counterpart in Canons B1 to B5 of the Revised Code of Canons.[1]

Some of us have doubted whether Canons were the most suitable mode of proceeding. But the Church of England has just spent 20 years in bringing its Canons up to date. It is clear to us that the Church intends to continue the use of this legislative form, in the appropriate fields marked out by the new Code. For this purpose it has set up a Standing Commission on Canon Law. Canons are not an antiquated form; they are used by other Anglican Churches to regulate spiritual matters. The experience of canon law revision has shown that the Royal Assent and Licence is no more than a formal requirement, so long as it is clear that the Canons are not repugnant to statute law or common law.[2] The way to enable the Church to legislate effectively by Canon in a particular ecclesiastical field is to repeal the statutes impinging on that field, and to make it clear, if necessary, that Canons can override any rules of ecclesiastical law or decisions of ecclesiastical courts in that field.

79 It therefore seems right that the new Measure should take the form of enabling the Church to order its worship by Canon or by the exercise

---

[1]Appendix A, paragraph 6.
[2]Appendix A, paragraphs 29 and 30.

of powers conferred by Canon, and should repeal the relevant Acts of Parliament and Measures. The most important of these are the Act of Uniformity, 1662, the Clerical Subscription Act 1865 (so far as it concerns worship) and the Prayer Book (Alternative and Other Services) Measure 1965. We set out in Appendix B a draft Measure on these lines, which not only covers the ordering of worship but some other related matters which we now consider.

AUTHORITY OVER DOCTRINE

The Canons in section A of the Revised Code, particularly Canon A5, set out the sources of doctrine in the Church of England.[1] These include the three historic formularies of the Thirty-nine Articles, the Book of Common Prayer and the Ordinal, to which the clergy are required to assent, on ordination and preferment, by the Clerical Subscription Act 1865. Because of this statutory requirement, which is reproduced in Canon C15, the three formularies cannot be altered without a Measure approved by Parliament.

This situation does not give the same cause for disquiet as the situation in respect of worship. We do not find any desire to alter the historic formularies. The report published in 1968 of the Archbishop's Commission on Christian Doctrine[2] rejected the idea of a revision of the Thirty-nine Articles, and recognised the difficulties of producing a new set of authoritative formularies. They recommended instead a new form of assent preceded by a preface which would interpret the formularies in their historical context and in relation to other Christian doctrines: see chapter 7 of their report.

We do not think that legislation on this subject should take the minimal form of amending the Declaration of Assent in the Clerical Subscription Act 1865, but that it should repeal the relevant provisions of that Act and leave the forms of subscription to doctrine to be prescribed by Canon alone. Indeed we think that there should be a rather wider power to interpret by Canon the historic formularies, not limited to prescribing the forms of assent.

We recommend that the Measure already proposed should empower the General Synod to prescribe by Canon the obligations of the clergy and certain lay officers to subscribe to the doctrine of the Church, and the forms of that subscription; and also to interpret by Canon the formularies of the Church.
    This recommendation is included in the draft Measure in Appendix B, which also provides for the repeal of the provisions of the Clerical Subscription Act 1865 relating to subscription to doctrine.

---

[1] Appendix A, paragraph 7.
[2] *Subscription and Assent to the Thirty-nine Articles, SPCK, 1968.*

84 Our recommendations with respect to forms of worship would cover matters dealt with in the rubrics of the Prayer Book that directly relate to the conduct of worship, because they form part of the actual services. But there are other matters contained in those rubrics (and in a few connected statutory provisions) which concern the services but are not part of them, e.g. vestures, qualifications for ordination, feasts and holy days, admission to Holy Communion, powers of lay persons to conduct services, the qualifications of godparents. All these matters are now included in the Revised Code of Canons, authority being given in some cases by a series of Measures which would themselves stand in the way of future amendments of the Canons concerned.[1] We believe that Parliament which, as we have shown, has expressed some sense of its unfitness to deal with matters of this kind, would agree that the Church should have power to deal with them by Canon and that the Measures concerned should be repealed.

85 One provision, however, was excluded from the Revised Code pending further consideration by the Church, namely, a provision for regulating the admission to Holy Communion of persons who had not been confirmed according to the Church of England rite. There is now before the General Synod a Measure conferring powers, in wide terms, for regulating this matter by Canon and regulations, notwithstanding the rubric at the end of the confirmation service. This Measure is in accordance with our recommendations.

86 *We recommend that the proposed Measure should empower the General Synod to amend or revoke by Canon the rubrics of the Book of Common Prayer, and to provide by Canon for any of the matters dealt with in those rubrics.*

This recommendation is also included in the draft Measure in Appendix B.[2]

---

[1]Appendix A, paragraph 29.
[2]See note of dissent to this Chapter on pages 85—87.

CHAPTER 3

Appointment of Bishops

Some people much object to the system whereby the Prime Minister nominates to the Crown the persons to be selected for election by a dean and chapter to be bishop. Other people think it the best of all systems.

We have felt the difficulty that another Commission, the Howick Commission, lately (1964) reported with unanimous conclusions. The Howick Commission was composed of members of the Church of England with widely differing opinions. Yet their conclusions were unanimous. Some of their conclusions however were not acceptable when they were discussed in the Church Assembly, and this was one reason which led to our Commission. We have not therefore been able to regard this matter as settled for the time being, but have considered it afresh. We have however had the benefit of the evidence available to the Howick Commission. If we come to different conclusions, that will be more because we form different opinions from the evidence than because we have different evidence to offer.

The Howick Commission left open the question whether the arrangements for the appointment of bishops might need modification if the Church of England were drawn into closer relation with other Churches. You have required us to take those future relations into consideration. The further evidence which we have taken, beyond the evidence offered to the Howick Commission, chiefly consists of evidence from Free Churchmen and Roman Catholics.

The Howick Commission unanimously recommended that the place of the Prime Minister in the system ought (with modifications) to continue. Opinions from other Churches pressed us that it ought on the contrary, to cease. The witnesses who were not members of the Church of England were unanimous in pressing us to recommend that it ought to cease.

Previous Commissions suggested that the disquiet was the result in some measure of ignorance of the extent to which the Church is consulted under the present system. But, whatever may have been the position in the past, the impression we form today is that those who are disquieted and uneasy are usually aware of the main features of the present arrangements, and that more detailed information often tends not to diminish but to increase their disquiet. The disquiet comes, many of us believe, not from any widely held belief that the present system produces anything but good bishops, but because it is felt to be inappropriate and unfitting in modern circumstances that the initiative in the appointment of the Church's chief pastors should be in the hands of the State, and that the Church ought to prefer a method of appointment which was 'open'. This said, we do not think that there is any great enthusiasm for elections and electoral systems as such ; and, indeed, the suggestion that an adoption of an alternative to the present system might lead to lobbying and canvassing causes many, particularly clergy, to shy away from change, while remaining unhappy about the present system.

DIOCESAN BISHOPRICS: THE PRESENT LAW AND PROCEDURE

92 The procedure for the appointment of diocesan bishops is laid down by the Appointment of Bishops Act 1533. The Act ensures that the effective power of appointment is in the hands of the Crown. It provides that when a see is vacant the Crown will grant a licence to the dean and chapter of the cathedral church to elect a new bishop and that the royal licence will be accompanied by a letter missive containing the name of the person whom they are to elect. When the election has taken place, Letters Patent are issued under the Great Seal to the archbishop of the province requiring him to confirm the appointment and, where necessary, to consecrate the bishop-elect.[1] The Act provided that the dean and chapter and the archbishop are to suffer the penalties of *Praemunire* if they fail to comply with Royal Commands. These penalties, long disused, have recently been abolished. The present position is therefore that the dean and chapter, if they now refuse to elect the Crown's nominee, will suffer no penalty under this Act. But they cannot elect a nominee of their own, and if they fail to act on the Crown's recommendation, the Crown could theoretically enforce its will by Letters Patent. On the other hand, the Archbishop can now refuse to consecrate the Crown's nominee without rendering himself liable to the penalties of *Praemunire*, and there is no substitute for consecration.

93 Behind this formal procedure, there has developed a complex informal procedure for the selection of the Crown's nominee, involving consultation of a wide range of persons and interests within the Church and outside it. All the evidence is that successive Prime Ministers in recent times have regarded their responsibilities in this respect as a matter of importance. But in the press of business today it would be unlikely for the Prime Minister personally to take the initiative in the routine of consultation as, for example, Mr Gladstone seems to have done. In the present century, the initiative in these matters has increasingly been taken, on the Prime Minister's behalf, by one of his

---

[1] In the diocese of Sodor and Man there is no chapter and the bishop is appointed by Letters Patent.

private secretaries, styled the Secretary for Appointments, who is a permanent civil servant. As the Howick Commission put it:

'As soon as it is known that a see is vacant or will shortly become vacant, the Prime Minister's Secretary for Appointments undertakes a series of consultations with the laity as well as with bishops and other clergy both within and outside the diocese. The widest possible information is sought and obtained in regard to the needs of the diocese as well as of the Church as a whole. This enquiry is made against the background of a continuous process of consultation and collation. Only thus can the Prime Minister exercise properly his personal responsibility for the nomination he makes to the Sovereign. Both at an early and at a late stage the respective Archbishop is consulted and the Archbishop of Canterbury is kept informed of developments in both provinces. At the final stage, the respective Archbishop gives the Prime Minister the names of two or three persons, indicating that the choice of any one of them would have his approval. (It will be understood that the names are names of persons whom the Archbishop knows (from the Prime Minister's Appointments Secretary) to be under serious consideration at that stage.) The Prime Minister who has at his disposal all the information afforded by the process of consultation is then in a position to consider his recommendation to the Sovereign for election by the dean and chapter.'[1]

Since the Howick Commission reported – indeed as a result of the implementation in part of its recommendations – the pattern of consultation has altered in two ways. Each diocese now has a Vacancy-in-See Committee, representative of the clergy and laity of the diocese, which meets – usually under the chairmanship of the suffragan bishop – to prepare a statement of the needs of the diocese for submission to the Prime Minister and the Archbishops. The Archbishops, for their part, have now appointed a layman to act as their Appointments Secretary. Unlike the Prime Minister's secretary he does not engage in consultations within the diocese when there is a vacancy but, like him, he engages in a continuous process of consultation so as to ensure that the Archbishops have available the fullest information about those who might be suitable for appointment to higher office. With his assistance, the Archbishops, from their knowledge of the Church and the clergy, are in a strong position both to suggest names to the Prime Minister for consideration and to comment upon the names which he decides to consider. If the Archbishop considered a person unsuitable as a bishop or for appointment to a particular see, he would make his views on the matter known to the Prime Minister's secretary at an early stage in the process of consultation. Our clear impression from the evidence we have received is that in modern circumstances there is no question of the Prime Minister proceeding with the recommendation of a person to whose appointment he knows the Archbishop

---

[1]*Crown Appointments and the Church*, p. 31, CIO, 1964.

to be entirely opposed. But this is not to say that the two or three persons from whom the final choice is made are necessarily the persons whom the Archbishop would himself have chosen or that the choice made necessarily accords with any preference the Archbishop may have expressed, though it often may.

95 The Commission thinks that some change is necessary but is divided on what we should recommend. We therefore propose to state two different recommendations side by side. The crux is whether the Prime Minister shall retain a part in the process of selection.

PROPOSAL A

96 The paragraphs which follow (97–116) contain the recommendations of one group in the Commission, and it is to them, not to the whole Commission, that the word 'we' refers in these paragraphs. The recommendations of a second group follow in paragraphs 117–133.

97 The alternative to the present system is some form of election. There are formidable arguments against election. The question was considered by two previous Commissions on Church and State – in 1935 and 1949 – and by the Howick Commission. All desired to see improvements in the machinery for consulting church opinion. None proposed the abolition of the ultimate Crown prerogative.

98 The view that the Church must be free to choose its own leaders is sometimes made to rest upon the assumption that the State is a purely secular authority divorced from spiritual concerns, separate from, if not actually opposed to, the interests of the Church. But this view of Church-State relationships has limited relevance to our present situation.

99 A modern democratic state represents in some sense the will of the people, albeit inadequately and with limitations. It is concerned not merely with the exercise of power over the people, but with their whole life, economic, social, cultural and spiritual; with the care of the sick and the old, the promotion of leisure activities and educational opportunity, with charity and compassion and social justice. The existence of a spiritual dimension in government reminds those in power that their influence is not confined to earthly or material things, but is concerned also with those affairs of men, in which their true humanity consists and in which, as Christians might say, they stand face to face with eternity. We believe that this dimension should be recognised and emphasised, and that a divorce between the interests of the Church and the interests of the State would damage both.

100 Ever since the disruption in the Church of Scotland (1843) great use has been made of the phrase 'the Crown rights of the Redeemer', and

the usual implication is that the Redeemer's rights in the Church are only fully recognised by a system of church appointments wholly governed by ecclesiastical machinery. Such a view may exaggerate the degree to which churchmen can be delivered from limitations in their perspective, and may underestimate the degree to which God's providence may work through agencies not strictly ecclesiastical.

Under the present system, bishops of the Church of England are more than diocesan pastors and senior members of the Church's organisation. Their views on ethical and moral issues are sought by many bodies and individuals at all levels of the national life, both publicly and privately. This interest is found far outside the number of those who belong to our Church. Far more people than the Anglicans in a bishop's diocese have a concern in the kind of man that he is. This is an important justification for a 'national' element in the system of appointment, that is, an element which represents the people generally and not only the members of the denomination.

The view that an electoral college is the right and proper body to choose church leaders also rests on the assumption that church organisation is fully representative. It is not. Though steps have been taken in this century to improve participation in church government, particularly by the representation of the laity, the Church is considerably less democratic in operation than the State. Like any other social grouping, the Church has different dimensions and degrees of membership. More than half of the population claim to be in some sense members of the Church. They are not necessarily represented by the small proportion whose names find their way onto the electoral roll. A series of filters operates in restricting participation in church government. The election of members of parochial church councils, or elections from deanery synods to General Synod, are as vulnerable as any political group to the operation of pressure groups, to the inertia exercised by established tradition, and to that decent reluctance to put oneself forward which is the hallmark of the Englishman in committee. The obligations of service in General Synod are such as to preclude unbiased representation of the laity. As long as the General Synod meets during the week, it will be dominated by the retired, the leisured and the professional classes. We do not know the present social composition of the House of Laity, but it is a fair guess that it does not, even today, contain the 5 per cent of working class members recommended by the Selborne Committee in 1918.

Representation in General Synod includes the over-weighting of one occupational group: the clergy; and of senior members of that group: the bishops. There are good and sufficient reasons why this should be so for the internal affairs of the Church; but the appointment of bishops is not solely an internal affair of the Church. To transfer the power to appoint bishops to a system in which the clergy are so heavily represented, the bishops themselves play so great a part, and the laity are so inadequately represented, would be to create a self-perpetuating system. A strong lay element in appointment is not unsuitable, particularly when the bishops, as consecrators, have the final say.

104 It is not argued that those who hold power in the organisation of the Church are undemocratic whether in their thinking or in operation. The Church is, and ought to be, deeply appreciative of their ungrudging expenditure of time, skill and energy on its behalf. Nor is it suggested that a strictly democratic form of representation in church government on the lines of parliamentary government would be either possible or desirable; but it is argued that ultimate control in the appointment of spiritual leaders with a responsibility for the nation may legitimately continue to rest with the Crown acting on the advice of the Prime Minister because the Crown and the Prime Minister, acting together, represent the Christian people of England in a way in which the organisation of the Church does not.

105 Some of your Commission go further, and say that the Prime Minister acts as representative and trustee for the nation, in the discharge of its duties to God and his Church. Some attach special importance to the role of the Monarch as Supreme Governor of the Church of England, in whose name these appointments are made. The Crown, on this view, is the keystone, binding the Church and nation.

106 The alternative to this is a system of election. In many areas of life elections are admirable ways of producing what is wanted. They are (almost always) accompanied by various forms of manoeuvring which it is not necessary here to specify, but which almost always include an element of partisanship. The office in question is a sacred office. And partisanship is more distasteful in choosing men for this office than in choosing them for any other. The Moberly Commission noted that 'the experience of the Church elsewhere in elections has not been a uniformly happy one. They have sometimes been productive of strife and division. They have not always resulted in the appointment of the best, or even of markedly suitable men'.[1] We have heard of the embarrassments resulting from electoral procedures even in well-governed, mature Churches. A recent election abroad involved no fewer than 32 counts. And even when elections work well (we confess that there are times and places where they work well) the outcome of the election is an officer more narrowly restricted to church organisation than is the English bishop.

107 Ecclesiastical elections tend to produce safe men. The Crown's participation has allowed the possibility of choosing men who are less safe. Great leaders are rare under any system. But it can at least be said

---

[1] *Church and State* (CA 1023), p. 44, CIO, 1952.

with confidence that the present system has produced some outstanding men, and that at least a few of those men would not have reached the episcopate through an electoral system. The Crown can show, and has shown, a freedom of choice that probably no other authority could or would display. It has also acted impartially in respecting the various schools of opinion within the Church of England and in maintaining its comprehensiveness.

The Moberly Commission on Church and State[1] wrote: 'It is generally agreed that no change short of "disestablishment" could deny to the State all share in the appointment of bishops'. We find at the moment no such general agreement. But we urge you seriously to weigh this point of view.

We have hitherto avoided the word 'establishment' because we find it difficult to define what it means. But it is rather easier to guess at the meaning of 'disestablishment'. 'Disestablishment' would be likely to include: (1) a severing of the organs of the State from all public connexions with Christianity; and (2) a measure of disendowment. Both these would entail loss to the effective work of the churches in this country.

If there is a risk that what is being asked for would entail either or both of these consequences, then responsible men will go carefully before they recommend any such course of action. If the complete exclusion of the Prime Minister were necessary to the life of the Church, then the risk must be run. But we think it absurd to say that such an exclusion is necessary to the life of the Church. To risk either 'disestablishment' or 'disendowment', or both, on the issue of election of bishops appears unwise and irresponsible; for in this matter the Church has sufficient safeguards.

The shorthand expression 'bishops are appointed by the Prime Minister' needs to be filled out. Prime Ministers have at one point a decisive function. But they do not work in a vacuum – they begin with suggestions emerging from the Church, and at last depend on the Church to consecrate.

The Prime Minister is not a free agent in this matter. In his advice to the Sovereign he is subjected to six important safeguards:

(a) public opinion is against any misuse of patronage and he of all men is peculiarly liable to the influence of public opinion;

(b) he can only recommend a person who has been ordained priest after rigorous testing by the authorities of the Church;

---

[1] P. 43.

(c) he does in fact recommend one person from a very small number of persons who have been approved by the Archbishops;

(d) the person whom he recommends must in practice be acceptable to the majority of the dean and chapter of the cathedral of the diocese concerned;

(e) the person whom he recommends to the Queen must after election be consecrated by other bishops.

113 We find it difficult to understand how in the face of all these safeguards the exercise of the present system can be regarded as other than a choice by the Church.

114 An informal system of consultation has developed as an adjunct of the formal constitutional process. It would be possible to improve this system of consultation and to write it into the constitutional process in such a way that Church opinion would be more adequately represented while the Crown prerogative was preserved. There are four stages in the making of an appointment: the ascertainment of candidates, short-listing, nomination and ratification. We propose that the first three of these procedures might be placed in the hands of a Church Advisory Committee under the chairmanship of the Archbishop of the Province.

Such a committee might consist of:

The Archbishop of the Province;

the other Archbishop or his nominee;

six members appointed by the General Synod of whom at least one should be a diocesan bishop and at least three should be laymen;

four members, two clergy and two lay, appointed by, but not necessarily from, the Vacancy-in-See Committee of the vacant diocese;

the dean or provost of the cathedral of the vacant diocese.

The procedure for the ascertainment of candidates would be construed as widely as possible. Members of the Committee could propose names, and other organisations, ecclesiastical or lay, would be able to propose names to them. It would be possible to conceive a system where (on the analogy of the appointment of Justices of the Peace) any citizen would have the right to propose a name. The Archbishop's Appointments Secretary, acting as secretary to the Committee, would carry out enquiries as directed. The Advisory Committee would make a short list, and, after further enquiries, propose two or more names for submission to the Prime Minister. As the State came to have confidence in the representative organs in the Church, it might become customary, as it has become customary in the case of suffragan bishops, for Prime Ministers to submit the first of a number of names submitted to them by the Church. The views of the Crown and the Prime Minister could be taken into account at all stages. The Crown prerogative would remain untouched in the sense that the Prime Minister made a final choice and the final submission to the Crown. We envisage that the bishop would need, as now, to be elected by representatives of the diocese. The dean and representatives of the chapter should be part of the electing body, which would doubtless be not unlike the present Vacancy-in-see Committee.

This proposal would retain the national interest in the choice of a bishop, and at the same time give a further formal place to the part of the Church in consultation.

We therefore base our view that the present system should be modified, and not abolished, upon the following:

(1) The safeguards for the Church's interests are as strong as in any other system that could be devised;

(2) The bishop, willy-nilly, has a 'national' aspect as well as a 'denominational' aspect;

(3) We value the public links between the nation and the Christian Churches. We think it unreasonable to put these links into question by a theologically unwarranted rigidity about the way in which bishops ought to be appointed.

(4) The system works; and we see no alternative likely to work as well.

PROPOSAL B

Once again, the word 'we' in paragraphs 121–133 refers to a group of members in the Commission and not to the whole Commission.

The case against the present system is, simply, that it is obviously inappropriate. The bishops hold a sacred office, concerned with religion and the things of the Spirit. They are the representative leaders of a religious society. The State is a secular state. Not only need the Prime Minister not be a member of the Church which the bishops are to serve. He need not even have an understanding of religion, let alone the wants of the Church of which he is helping to choose the leaders. Of course he has usually had both these qualifications. But he need not have them.

In past ages in England Church and society were more nearly identical. Citizen and churchman could then in theory be identified. Our system is an historical relic of those ages. It depends upon an axiom about English society which was once true or nearly true, and is now not true. It has served a useful purpose in the past. It has outlived the age when it corresponded to reality. It ought to cease.

120 If it ought to cease, arguments about whether it works well, or whether some other system would produce better results, or worse, are irrelevant. That other systems work reasonably well is proved by the experience of all other Churches in the Anglican Communion.

121 We think that the present system has demerits.

(a) The authorities of the Church are consulted as a matter of courtesy, not of right. The system depends on the goodwill and integrity of individuals. Can we be sure that it will always be so? While responsibility nominally rests with the Crown, actual responsibility lies with the Prime Minister, who is accountable neither to Parliament (where he cannot be questioned about ecclesiastical appointments since these are matters affecting the Crown prerogative) nor to the Church. We are very dependent on a few people continuing to act with the integrity which they show at the moment; and the choice of these few people depends on national considerations quite outside the purview of the Church, and sometimes upon the accidents of political circumstance.

(b) The apparent lack of accountability gives rise to unease. The system depends on confidential communication, specially through the Prime Minister's Secretary for Appointments upon whom the day-to-day work largely devolves. Any system of confidential consultation carried on mainly with individuals is bound to lead some to believe that good men have gone unnoticed and that others have been unfairly denied preferment. The fact that the Prime Minister and those who advise him necessarily stand aside from the main stream of the Church's life was formerly seen as an advantage, but some of us would question this. Anyone specialising in a particular class of appointment (and there have been only three holders of the office of Secretary for Appointments in the last thirty years) must in the course of time develop working assumptions about the qualities to be looked for in candidates for particular appointments, and after some time may not be sufficiently responsive to the changing needs of the Church. No system (of course) could be infallible. But this system is shrouded in privacy, and is believed by many to be less 'open' even than it is.

We receive bishops by a process, and nothing is known about an important part of the process. The world is beginning to prefer 'open' methods in the choice of such representative persons as bishops must necessarily be.

(c) It is fairly claimed for the present system that in the past it made possible some bold appointments. We wonder whether it is not also marked by a uniformity of selection in the matter of social background, education and training.

(*d*) The system of consultation left much to be desired until recently, and still leaves something to be desired. Until the advent of the Vacancy-in-See Committees, it depended entirely upon consultation with individuals. These individuals might be chosen haphazardly. Doubtless they included (for two centuries at least) the Archbishop of Canterbury, and in recent times also the Archbishop of York. But even the Archbishops gave their views as individuals. There was no corporate expression of opinion by any body in the Church, before the election by the dean and chapter, which until recently stood under threat of penalty if it expressed any opinion contrary to that of the Crown.

The matter is improved by the Vacancy-in-See Committees. These Committees give vigorous expression to the opinion of the diocese, and their view weighs the more heavily because it is corporately expressed. But it is unsatisfactory that the diocese should be able to utter a representative voice while the Church at large cannot. The diocesan element in the choice of a bishop is beginning to preponderate over the national element. The bishop is not only a bishop of his diocese. His office and work are as a bishop in the Church of God, and the Church beyond the diocese has a legitimate concern in the choice.

We acknowledge that the proposals in paragraph 114 go some way towards removing these defects, but they would still leave the Prime Minister with an effective power of choice between candidates, and this we regard as unacceptable.

We are not impressed by the argument that a bishop's position in the nation is enhanced by the present arrangements. On the contrary we are sure that the reputation of the Church of England suffers with some people because such a sentence as this (however crude in formulation) can be said: 'The Prime Minister, though he need not be a Christian, appoints the bishops of the Church of England'.

Among those with whom its reputation suffers are all the Free Churches; and the established Church of Scotland. The Free Church representatives, whom we consulted, made it clear that their traditions could not tolerate such an arrangement as ours, and that they strongly dislike it. They would find it unacceptable to be joined in a united Church of which the leaders were nominated by the Crown on ministerial invitation and advice.

For these reasons we need to find a system of electing bishops by representatives of the Church.

We now go on to suggest an electoral system. But we must make it clear that our view of the need for such a system does not depend upon which system is chosen. We are more concerned that bishops of the Church of England should be chosen by the Church of England, than that they should be elected in the particular way which we are about to suggest.

125 We recognise that electoral systems have their difficulties. But there is ample evidence in the experience of all the other Churches of the Anglican Communion that these systems work reasonably well. And we were not surprised to be told by representatives of other Provinces, whom we consulted at the time of the 1968 Lambeth Conference, that they would not, even if they could, wish for such a system of appointments as we have.

126 The possibilities may conveniently be grouped into three categories. These are:—

    (i) Election by a diocesan electoral college.

    (ii) Election by an electoral college made up of representatives of the province and the diocese.

    (iii) Election by a small electoral board.

(I) AND (II) ELECTION BY A DIOCESAN OR PROVINCIAL ELECTORAL COLLEGE

127 These methods – election by a provincial or diocesan electoral college – are the basis of the methods of appointment in use in most of the other Anglican provinces. In the Episcopal Church in Scotland, bishops are elected by diocesan colleges; in the Church in Wales, there is a provincial college; and the Church of Ireland, which adopted on disestablishment the diocesan system, has now gone over to the provincial. To secure a body of electors sufficiently representative and well informed, most provinces make provision for a membership of at least fifty persons. In some cases clergy and laity meet and vote together; in other cases they meet in separate houses. It is usually open to any member of the college, or any two members, to suggest a name or names for consideration. In some cases the other bishops, as well as their right to refuse to consecrate, have a formal right of veto.

128 Opinions differ about the success, or otherwise, of these electoral systems. In previous reports, and in this report, reference has been made to the difficulties to which such a system gives rise, to the possibility of lobbying and the risk that such systems might exacerbate party differences. Fears have been expressed that some clergy might be reluctant to submit themselves to the processes of election. Cases are occasionally reported where an electoral college is deadlocked or only reaches a conclusion after many ballots. Our impression is that the practical and other difficulties are less than have sometimes been supposed and that for the most part electoral procedures work satisfactorily – and in a way which, contrary to the suggestion often made in the past, the participants find edifying.

129 There is, however, a general view that of these two methods of election, provincial and diocesan, the former is much to be preferred. A diocesan electorate tends to know only its own clergy, and finds it

difficult to draw upon outside information. A provincial college is likely to be better informed, and at the same time bears testimony in its composition that bishops belong not only to the individual diocese but to the Church at large.

Short of direct election, which we take to be impracticable, a system of electing bishops by a provincial college is in theory the system which, in modern circumstances, gives most apt expression to the desire of Church people to participate in responsibility for the choice of their chief pastors. We do not, however, recommend it for adoption in England in the foreseeable future, though some of us consider that in time such a system will come to be adopted here. We reject it now for essentially practical reasons. We have to find a system which can be applied efficiently, and with reasonable economy of time, in two provinces and 43 dioceses. On average, about three or four dioceses become vacant each year. The bringing together of large bodies of electors on three or four separate occasions would place a heavy burden on those concerned. The problems would be intensified if the Church decided in favour of more, or smaller, dioceses. Again, selection has been made hitherto on a national basis, with opportunity for consideration of the widest possible field of candidates. We think it desirable that these elements should be preserved in the new system, and that the Church would stand to lose if they were not. Moreover on general grounds the Church would stand to do better to adopt a system similar to the old, but in its own hands, than to launch out upon a totally different and untried system.

(iii) ELECTION BY AN ELECTORAL BOARD

We have therefore come to the conclusion that a better way would be to entrust the choice to a small electoral board representative of the Church as a whole and of the individual diocese. The electoral board would be vested with the responsibility which, under the present system, falls to the Prime Minister and his advisers. In terms of numbers the maximum membership should, we think, be about twelve. Such a board might consist of:—

the Archbishop of the Province;

the other Archbishop – or his nominee;

six members – appointed by the General Synod of whom at least one should be a diocesan bishop and at least three should be laymen;

four members – two clergy, two lay appointed by but not necessarily from the Vacancy-in-See Committee.

The dean or provost of the cathedral would sit as a non-voting assessor.[1]

---

[1] It will be observed that the suggested composition of the Committee in paragraph 114 is virtually the same as that of the Electoral Board in paragraph 131 above.

132 We see many advantages in the system we propose. It would allow the blending of some of the best features of the old system, the possibility of full and confidential consultation about candidates who would be drawn from the widest possible range, with the principle of free choice by the Church of its chief pastors. We cannot see that there would be any practical problems inherent in its operation which could not easily be overcome. Hence we are in favour of a small board as opposed to the larger bodies of electors generally found in other Anglican provinces.

133 What of the view of the constitutional position held by our predecessors and by some of our colleagues? Is it realistic to suppose that the State would be willing to concede to the Church the right to elect its own bishops in some such manner as we have suggested? We think that it is. We find it difficult to believe that nowadays the State, in the person of the Prime Minister of the day, has any great interest, as a matter of public concern, in appointments to diocesan bishoprics, even though the bishop in question may in due course take his place in the House of Lords. If we are right in thinking that the State's interest in episcopal appointments has declined, it is hard to imagine that the participation of the Prime Minister in the selection process would now be regarded as the *sine qua non* on which the Church's tenure of its historic endowments would depend for its continuance. On the other hand, Parliament might wish to feel, before approving the legislation, that the arrangements proposed were sensible and practicable, and that there is satisfactory provision for representation of bishops, clergy and laity and for consultation. We suggest that a small electoral board such as we have proposed, on which the Archbishops would sit, and whose membership is likely to consist of clerical and lay representatives chosen by the General Synod and the diocese, would be the kind of body to which Parliament would feel it appropriate to transfer the task of selection, especially if provision were made for full consultation within the Church and outside it.

134 We recognise of course that the power to be transferred is a power formally of the Crown, even though it is exercised on the advice of the Prime Minister. Many members of the Church would feel it fitting that the Sovereign should continue to be associated with the process of election in a symbolic continuance of the procedure at the ratification stage whereby the nomination is formally made by the Crown. We acknowledge that it would not be easy, from the constitutional standpoint, to reconcile this with our recommendation that the effective choice should pass from ministerial hands. But the British constitution has proved remarkably adaptable, and what one generation has considered constitutionally impracticable has frequently been found feasible by the next. We are confident that here, as elsewhere, a solution acceptable to all could, with goodwill, be achieved.

135 We therefore recommend that the part of the Prime Minister ought to cease, for the following reasons:
(1) It is inappropriate in the context of modern England.

(2) It offends some members of the Church.

(3) It helps to identify the Church with the (colloquial) 'establishment'.

(4) Reunion with anyone is impossible unless it ceases.

(5) We see no reason to think that other systems would not work well.

On this issue the Commission is divided. We have given to each side the opportunity to make recommendations. We leave these differing recommendations for the decision of the Church.[1]

SUFFRAGAN BISHOPS

The present arrangement for the appointment of suffragan bishops is described in Appendix A (paragraph 10). The bishop of the diocese submits two names to the Crown. By convention the Prime Minister endorses the first name. Thus the effective choice rests with the diocesan who is not obliged to seek any advice before making his nominations, though generally (not, we understand, invariably) the diocesan will consult the Archbishop and other persons, including the Prime Minister's Secretary for Appointments and the Archbishops' Appointments Secretary.

The Howick Commission thought that, since the choice and appointment of suffragan bishops is of concern to the whole Church and not only to the particular diocese and diocesan, this system should be modified so that in future the Archbishops and the diocesan should decide together on the nomination to be made, with only one name going forward in the Petition to the Crown. We share the Howick Commission's view that the power to nominate should not be exercised by the diocesan acting alone, bearing in mind that a suffragan may well find himself working with more than one diocesan in the course of his tenure, and that there is a tendency for suffragans to become diocesans. Since the Howick Commission reported, there has been a further development. In one or two larger dioceses the suffragan has been given a jurisdiction almost equal to the jurisdiction of a diocesan. In such dioceses, the single diocesan bishop is alone, or may be alone, in choosing two or three other men who will bear the effective responsibility of a diocesan bishop. Even in the normal diocese, where this does not happen, the suffragan is more than the personal assistant of the diocesan. He is a bishop of the whole Church. Present practice certainly needs modifying.

---

[1]Without necessarily accepting all the arguments of paragraphs 97–116 for Proposal A, the following signatories of the Report recommend that proposal:

The Bishop of Chester, the Bishop of Leicester, the Dean of Chester, the Archdeacon of Swindon, Mr Justice Cumming-Bruce, Professor Chadwick, Professor Jones, Sir Timothy Hoare.

The following signatories of the Report recommend Proposal B:

The Earl of March, the Archdeacon of Westminster, Canon Westwood, Lady Ogilvie, Mr Pattinson.

The three members who are not signatories, Miss Pitt, Mr Cornwell and Mr Coe would, if they had to choose, prefer Proposal B.

139 How the present practice is modified depends upon the mode of proceeding in regard to diocesan bishops. We are agreed that no one should be elected a suffragan without the consent of the diocesan. But we think that the appointment should follow the way which is chosen in the case of diocesan bishops. If either of the two modifications described above were adopted, the same method would be used for suffragans. In one case the Church Advisory Committee, with the diocesan bishop sitting upon it, would recommend a name or two names to the Crown through the Prime Minister. In the other case the Electoral Board, with the diocesan bishop sitting upon it, would choose a single name and forward it directly to the Crown. In either method the consent of the diocesan bishop should be necessary to the appointment.

140 The present practice is so obviously in need of modification that we hope its amendment will not have to wait until the Church has decided how to move in the matter of choosing diocesan bishops.

SUPPLEMENTARY SUGGESTIONS
141 In order to keep as simple as possible the issue between the two alternative proposals for the appointment of diocesan bishops, some supplementary suggestions on matters of detail, including modifications in the case of vacancies in archbishoprics, are added in Appendix C. Reference is also made in that Appendix to Crown patronage of other offices in the Church.

CHAPTER 4

The House of Lords

The constitutional development of the House of Lords is a matter for the State and not the Church. We refrain from intruding our ideas upon the general subject.

But we need to make two remarks upon it nevertheless; first because our opinion upon the subject is expected; and secondly because, if the Church wished that the responsibility of the Prime Minister in advising the Crown on the nomination of bishops should end, it would create a new situation about their seats in the House of Lords.

At present there are 43 diocesan bishops. The two Archbishops and the Bishops of London, Winchester and Durham occupy seats *ex officio*; the next 21 bishops hold seats in accordance with the seniority of their appointment. All hold their seats only during the tenure of their sees. They are not 'life peers', but 'lords spiritual' while they hold their office.

The White Paper on the reform of the House of Lords[1] suggested on the one hand that a reformed House of Lords could be argued to be 'an essentially secular institution' and on the other hand that the history of the House of Lords, and the special place of the Church of England within the constitution, warranted the continuation of the seats of bishops. Since the White Paper proposed that the size of the House, and especially its voting size, should be diminished, it proposed that the number of bishops in the House be reduced, by a gradual method, to 16; but of these 16 only the two Archbishops and the three senior bishops should have automatic voting rights. Under the White Paper, any new bishop should have leave to refuse the offer of a seat and membership would then devolve upon the next most senior bishop; and any bishop possessing a seat (except the two Archbishops and the three senior bishops) could retire from his seat, and make room for another willing to serve. The two Archbishops and the three senior bishops should be exempt from the new requirement that they must attend a minimum number of sittings if they were to exercise their rights to vote.

The result which the White Paper reached, and the methods which it recommended to attain the objective, were generally accepted by

---

[1]Cmnd 3799, November, 1968.

bishops and others at the time; and this Commission sees no reason to recommend any change in the view that the proposals, or proposals of this kind, should be accepted in the context of a general reduction in the size of the House of Lords.

147 But it is possible to be more critical of the philosophy underlying the White Paper. For it appeared to present the alternative; either a secular institution, or provision for bishops. It does not envisage seats for religious leaders other than bishops of the Church of England.

148 We are not sure what is meant by the argument that a reformed House of Lords should be an 'essentially secular institution'. In its development since 1911 the Upper House has played a useful part in the body politic, in this way among other ways, by securing a voice in Parliament for various interests in the country which are less easy to secure by the normal process of election. Under the system of life peers leading members of trade unions and industry and the universities and the medical profession are given places from which they may speak. In a different way the Law Lords speak for another important area of the national life. The religious groups of Britain are quite as significant in the national life as other groups.

149 In consulting our witnesses, we have found a very common opinion that the House of Lords is a place where religious leaders ought to be able to speak. In the House of Lords they can retain their independence and avoid a party whip. One speaker in the parliamentary debates upon this question criticised the presence of the bishops on the ground that they were there only to represent the interests of a particular denomination. But this view of why bishops are there we did not find among our witnesses. We found that many non-Anglicans valued their presence in the Lords as speaking for a large body of Christian opinion in this country.

150 Three or four members of this Commission think that, in both Houses of Parliament, those who are elected or chosen for other reasons than religion, but happen also to be religious men, will be the right people to speak on moral or general issues from the point of view of the Churches. The majority of us follow the opinion, which we have found to be widespread, that some men should sit in the House of Lords specially because in so doing they are able to speak as members of Churches.

151 In the plan of the White Paper the number of members of the whole House was to be reduced and therefore the number of bishops was to be reduced. We hope that in any future reconstruction such a reduction of bishops' seats, or some other method, would make available seats for leaders from other Churches.

152 (a) If the less radical proposal about bishops in the last chapter were adopted, the matter would then go forward as the White Paper

proposed, that is, with a fixed number of seats for bishops of the Church of England, *ex officio* according to seniority (but with power to each bishop to decline to serve, as suggested within the White Paper) and with seats for other religious leaders occupied by 'life peers'.

(*b*) If the more radical proposal about bishops in the last chapter were adopted, it would naturally throw into question the method which distinguishes the appointment of bishops to seats in the House of Lords from the appointment of members of other religious groups by life peerages. Perhaps the State might wish to continue the existing arrangement, partly for historical reasons, as a still useful way of securing that the leaders of the Church of England might have a place from which to speak. Perhaps the State would simply choose persons to serve as representatives of religion and, so far as bishops were chosen, they would be chosen by the Crown from among those persons whom the Church of England had elected as bishops. They would no longer serve by seniority of consecration but because they were invited to serve in Parliament by the Crown.

We have considered the possibility, which was suggested by more than one speaker in the debates in Parliament, of naming certain other offices in the Churches of Britain, besides diocesan bishoprics in the Church of England, which would *ex officio* qualify a man or woman for a seat in the House of Lords. In the House of Lords debates it was argued that for other denominations than the Church of England, many of whom have changing presidents or moderators, it would be better done by choice of particular persons; and, while being content with an *ex officio* system, we are inclined to agree with them.

We know that this speculates about the future. But the suggestion that this Commission might make proposals was made more than once in the parliamentary discussion. We do not wish the Church of England now to tie itself to any detailed scheme like the above, out of relation to an existing situation or proposal for parliamentary reform.

We think that there ought to be leaders of the Churches within a reformed House of Lords.

We recommend that others, besides bishops of the Church of England, should be chosen for this purpose.

Meanwhile the Crown, without waiting for any reconstruction of the House of Lords, could continue to secure the representation of other Churches by using the system of life peerages. We hope that it will.

CHAPTER 5

Organisation and Property

156 A large number of the laws of the Church deal with its institutions and organisation; ecclesiastical offices and duties attaching; the patronage system; stipends, pensions and endowments; church building; and benefice property. Because most of the law in this field is statute law and common law, it can only be altered by Act of Parliament, or by Measure approved by Parliament.

157 In the Disestablishment Act for the Welsh Church of 1914, all the laws of the Church were in effect converted into the rules and trusts of a voluntary society. If that were to happen to the Church of England, the Church would be able to change most of these laws without reference to Parliament. But many of the laws do affect private property, or the destination of trusts, where Parliament is rightly concerned. No one feels that in this area Parliament is interfering in matters which solely concern the Church. In some of the more thorny and complex of these problems of property a disestablished Church would need to go to Parliament, and would do it with less ease if it had not our present system of being able to promote Measures through Parliament. We find little or no discontent about the principle of our system. And we find that the attempts to convert all the laws of the Church into the rules and trusts of a voluntary society would involve a drastic operation not likely to command such wide support in Church, Parliament or nation as to make it practicable.

158 But if we find no discontent about the principle, we find discontent, especially among our parliamentarians, about the practice which requires such frequent recourse to Parliament for changes (sometimes minor changes) in the Measures concerning the property of the Church. They complain that the Church, having inherited so much public law in the course of its history, has to agree and promote so many Measures for which parliamentary approval must be sought.

159 The Enabling Act of 1919 conferred great benefits upon the Church. Without it the Church of England would, like other Churches (but much more than other Churches) need to proceed by private Bill, because only on rare and special occasions can parliamentary time now be found for public Bills on church matters. Certainly we much prefer the procedure of Church Assembly Measure to that of private Bill.

The obvious way of amending the Enabling Act would be to substitute some form of 'negative resolution' for the present requirement of 'affirmative resolution' by both Houses. That is, a Measure would after a certain period become law if no one in either House objected to it. We do not recommend this change, because we doubt on principle whether Measures should have the status of Acts of Parliament, and should repeal and amend public Acts and laws, without having received the affirmative approval of Parliament.

The only other way of proceeding is to survey the laws of the Church that concern property and organisation, and to examine ways of reducing the need for future legislation by Measure. There is the possibility that by simplifying the law, and reframing Measures so as to give wider administrative powers and powers of subordinate legislation, we should have far less need for subsequent amendment by Measure. This would accord with the trend of the last half century in secular legislation, which leaves much of the detail of statutory provision to be covered by regulations or administrative powers.

The Constitution of the General Synod[1] sets out in Article 6 the various ways in which the General Synod can 'make provision' concerning the Church of England. These include (1) Canons, (2) Measures, (3) subordinate legislation under Measures or Canons, and (4) direct provision by the Synod in cases where legislative provision is not required. This last method needs to be used much more than it is. With these possibilities in mind we have considered the statutes and laws affecting the organisation and property of the Church.

SYNODS AND PAROCHIAL CHURCH COUNCILS

The Synodical Government Measure 1969 has already gone a little way in the direction which we wish. Without further reference to a Measure, the General Synod can now amend the rules by which members of the House of Laity, or of diocesan and deanery synods, or of parochial church councils, are elected. In the past such amendment has three times required recourse to Parliament for a Measure. It will no longer need such recourse.[2] The Synod may also extend, amend or define the functions of diocesan or deanery synods as laid down by the Synodical Government Measure.

But we observe a habit of mind which prefers to work through Measure. For example, the General Synod and diocesan synods do their administrative work through boards, councils, and other bodies responsible to

---

[1] Cf Appendix A, paragraph 35.

[2] The new power of amendment is in section 7 of the Synodical Government Measure and applies to the rules in Schedule 3; the amendments are subject to the negative resolution procedure in Parliament. The original Rules for the Representation of the Laity, contained in the Schedule to the Constitution of the Church Assembly, were completely re-enacted by Measure, with amendments on each occasion, in 1929, 1956 and lastly in the Synodical Government Measure itself.

them. Many of these bodies, especially when they are diocesan, labour with a constitution and functions defined in detail by Measures; with the result that administrative changes require amending Measures in Parliament. The reason may have been to give a statutory status to the bodies concerned, or to secure uniformity in administration between the various dioceses. We recommend that this reasoning be looked at critically in the future. Any Measure which in this area makes such provisions that alterations later would require another Measure, ought henceforth to be suspect.

TERRITORIAL ORGANISATION

165 The Pastoral Measure 1968 contains a new code, replacing a multitude of previous Acts and Measures, which gives power to provide by pastoral schemes:

(a) for altering diocesan boundaries, but not creating or abolishing dioceses;

(b) for creating, dissolving and altering benefices and parishes, and also archdeaconries and rural deaneries.

The schemes are initiated in the dioceses concerned, prepared by the Church Commissioners and confirmed by Order in Council.

Schemes under the Measure may deal with a number of other matters, including the designation and provision of parish churches and parsonages, the closing of redundant churches and churchyards, the adjustment of patronage rights and endowments. They thus provide a fairly comprehensive apparatus for altering the territorial structure of the Church without recourse to Parliament.

166 In one important respect, however, the apparatus is incomplete, in that it does not enable dioceses to be created or abolished. Between 1836, when the Ecclesiastical Commissioners were set up, and 1918, 16 new dioceses were created by Order in Council under the authority of an Act of Parliament setting out the boundaries of the new dioceses in detail. Since the Church Assembly was set up four more dioceses have now been created by Measure and Order in Council in the same way. We see every reason to expect that from time to time the Church of England will need to subdivide or to amalgamate dioceses. It would be reasonable for a new Measure to give powers to the General Synod to establish new dioceses and abolish old ones under schemes of the Church Commissioners confirmed by Order in Council.

THE CHURCH COMMISSIONERS

167 The Church Commissioners are a statutory corporation whose constitution and powers are laid down by statute. The constitution is mostly contained in the Church Commissioners Measure 1947, which amalgamated the Ecclesiastical Commissioners and Queen Anne's

Bounty. Section 6 of the Measure was re-enacted in 1964, so as to provide for the constitution of the two main executive committees. The appointment of the three Church Estates Commissioners, who play a key role, is still made under the Ecclesiastical Commissioners Act 1850.

The constitution reflects the history of the Church Commissioners and their predecessors, especially the Ecclesiastical Commissioners whose independent position was essential for the carrying out of reforms that were unpopular in some quarters of the Church. On the Government side, the general body of Commissioners includes high officers of State and of the judiciary, although their position is now a formal one; the First and Second Church Estates Commissioners are appointed by the Crown, and the Second Commissioner is in practice a member of the House of Commons; the accounts of the Commissioners are audited by the Comptroller and Auditor General, and their annual report and accounts are laid before Parliament; parliamentary questions are answered on behalf of the Commissioners by the Second Church Estates Commissioner in the House of Commons, or by a Church Commissioner (e.g. a diocesan bishop) in the House of Lords.

On the Church side the important features of the constitution are:

(a) The Chairman of the Board of Governors is the Archbishop of Canterbury, the majority of the members are bishops and clergymen, and six of the eight lay members (other than the Church Estates Commissioners and co-opted members) are chosen from those appointed by the General Synod.

(b) Apart from *ex officio* members, the majority of the members of the two main committees are chosen from those appointed by the Board of Governors or the Archbishop of Canterbury.

(c) The Third Church Estates Commissioner is appointed by the Archbishop of Canterbury, and all three Church Estates Commissioners are *ex officio* members of the General Synod.

(d) The annual report and accounts are laid before the General Synod.

The Government element in this constitution does not present any special problem for us. No one suggests that the Church Commissioners are influenced in the peformance of their functions by anything other than the interests of the Church. At the same time we do not think that this is a proper subject for delegated power of legislation by the General Synod. The constitution should only be amendable by Measure.

The present functions of the Church Commissioners fall into three main categories:

(1) territorial reorganisation at all levels, as the scheme-making authority under the Pastoral Measure 1968, including ancillary functions in respect of churches, endowments and patronage,

(2) managing the central endowments of the Church and applying the income, broadly speaking, to the payment of stipends and pensions of the clergy, and towards the provision and maintenance of certain categories of church buildings,

(3) supervising, as a consenting authority, dealings in benefice and other church property.

The endowments are managed under a great many Statutes and Measures, going back to Queen Anne and including a number of important Measures of recent years which improve the machinery of management and extend the purposes for which the funds may be applied.[1] We do not recommend that the statutory provisions should be made amendable otherwise than by Measure, but there is an obvious case for gathering them together (or most of them) in a single comprehensive Measure. In the process the powers might be simplified and drawn more widely, and so avoid occasions for future legislation. We recognise, however, that legislation of this kind would present many difficulties, raise large issues of policy, and require much consideration.

ECCLESIASTICAL COURTS

172 This subject is now mainly covered by the Ecclesiastical Jurisdiction Measure 1963.[2] For practical purposes the jurisdiction of ecclesiastical courts is limited to disciplinary proceedings against bishops and clergy, and faculty proceedings. Both classes of proceedings may give rise to questions of doctrine, ritual or ceremonial, and it was a main purpose of the 1963 Measure to secure that such questions should be decided by courts where the members of the courts were members of the Church. The Measure was the result of long consideration by the Church and was accepted by Parliament with little opposition. The State is concerned with the administration of justice, especially where there is a penal element, even by domestic tribunals. For example, the disciplinary tribunals of the medical and solicitors' professions are regulated by the Medical Act 1956 and the Solicitors Acts 1957 to 1965, and an appeal lies, in the first case, to the Judicial Committee of the Privy Council and, in the second case, to the High Court. *A fortiori*, disciplinary proceedings in the Church of England, administered at all levels by courts which have long been regarded as public courts, can rightly be the subject of statutory provision.

173 We hope that the Measure of 1963, replacing a large number of previous Acts and Measures, will last in substance for some time. Some

---

[1]The main original purpose for which the common fund of the Ecclesiastical Commissioners could be used under section 67 of the Ecclesiastical Commissioners Act 1840 was 'additional provision . . . for the cure of souls in parishes where such assistance is most required', and the similar original purpose of Queen Anne's Bounty was 'the augmentation of the maintenance of the poor clergy'. An account of the present situation with regard to the payment of stipends is given in the Report of the Commission on the Deployment and Payment of the Clergy, and brings out its complexity. *Partners in Ministry*, Chapter VII.

[2]For which see Appendix A, paragraph 17.

doubt about its detailed provisions, however, arises from the elaborate nature and expense of proceedings under the Measure, which recently aroused criticism. It looks as though it needs amendment.

ADMINISTRATION OF THE CLERGY

Section C of the Revised Code of Canons contains the rules concerning ordination and consecration; provides for the institution and licensing of ministers; and lays down the duties and rules affecting the various ecclesiastical offices. Our recommendation in chapter 2 covers the first of these subjects, which is linked with the ceremonies of ordination and consecration, and so would give power to the Church to alter the law on this subject by Canon, without recourse to Parliament. We think that similar provision should be made for other matters falling within Section C of the Revised Code, matters which at present are regulated by statutory provisions as well as by Canons, and so cannot be altered without a Measure. Some but not all of these matters arose in the course of canon law revision and Measures had to be passed before the Canons could be made. This dual process is very laborious and could arise in the future in other matters where statute and Canon overlap, e.g. the rules governing the residence and occupations of ministers, which can appropriately and simply be dealt with by Canon but are the subject of elaborate provisions in the Pluralities Act 1838. The solution is to repeal the statutes and leave the field clear for legislation by Canon alone.[1]

THE PATRONAGE SYSTEM

The patronage system was one of the first ecclesiastical subjects of parliamentary legislation (Statute of Westminster the Second, 1285), and since then there has been much legislation. In recent years Church Assembly Measures virtually provided for the abolition of the sale of advowsons, and gave to parishes a voice in the choice of incumbents, and by these two important reforms diminished the rights of patrons. The Pastoral Measure 1968 conferred powers to alter and suspend patronage rights by scheme or order, in consequence of parochial reorganisation. This proved to be the one feature of the Pastoral Measure on which the Ecclesiastical Committee felt considerable difficulty, for here the rights of the individual are plainly in question. We do not think that there can be any question of giving a general power to the Church to legislate on this subject without recourse to Measure in Parliament. Nor, at this stage, when the general question of patronage is under consideration, does it seem profitable to consider ways of simplifying the law. The recent recommendations of the Commission

---

[1]We have in mind, for example, the duties involved in the cure of souls; permission for clergy, ordained overseas, to officiate in England; collation, presentation, institution, and induction; licensing of ministers and curates; the declaration against simony; residence of incumbents; rules on whether the clergy may engage in other occupations.

on the Payment and Deployment of the Clergy,[1] which devised a new system for appointment, would have required implementation by Measure if they had proved acceptable to the Church. If there were further reconsideration of the general system of patronage, we hope that those responsible will remember our desire that the law should be simplified and that the application of new methods should not be embodied in statutory provisions which would later require statutory change.

PENSIONS OF THE CLERGY

176 It is generally thought to have been a mistake to embody all the detail of clergy pension schemes in Measures, of which there have been no less than sixteen. It would be perfectly possible to remedy this mistake by making the main Measure of 1961, as amended by two small Measures passed since then, amendable by scheme prepared by the Church of England Pensions Board and approved by the General Synod.

We recommend that powers to this effect should be given by a short enabling Measure. Pensions of local government officers and officers of other statutory bodies are provided under schemes or regulations made under statutory powers, and there is no reason why clergy pensions should not be in the same position.

BENEFICE AND PAROCHIAL PROPERTY

177 The property vested in the incumbent of a benefice as a spiritual corporation sole usually comprises the parsonage house and glebe and in most cases the church and churchyard. Churches and churchyards, because they are consecrated, differ from other benefice property. One of the effects of consecration is to set the building or ground apart for consecrated uses for ever, and so to prevent it being sold or leased for secular uses. For this reason the problem of powers of disposal, which looms large in the legislation affecting other benefice property, only arises when the church becomes redundant or the churchyard is no longer used for burial. At that point the powers exercisable by scheme under the Pastoral Measure 1968, which include power to remove the legal effects of consecration, come into operation, and appear to give sufficient liberty of action.

178 The vesting of the parsonage house and glebe in the incumbent as a corporation sole has resulted in a legal situation of rigidity and inconvenience. It compares unfavourably with the situation in other Churches whose church buildings are usually vested in trust corporations with sufficiently wide powers to enable them to mortgage and dispose of buildings and use the proceeds to improve or replace the buildings, and with sufficient resources to secure adequate maintenance. The incumbent's only powers of mortgage and disposal are those conferred by

---

[1]*Partners in Ministry*, Chapter 11, in particular pp. 27–31.

statutory provision. Historically, maintenance of the benefice property has depended upon the resources of the individual incumbent and the law of ecclesiastical waste. These have needed to be supplemented by statutory provisions for preventing dilapidations.

There has thus arisen a body of statute law giving to the incumbent powers to mortgage and dispose of parsonage house and glebe, and providing for their maintenance. The code of laws is elaborate and confusing.[1] It seems to us that most of these Acts and Measures could be replaced by a single comprehensive Measure, in which the powers could be broadly and simply defined if they were made subject to the consent of the appropriate authorities. An even simpler solution, if it were acceptable to the clergy, would be to vest parsonage houses and glebe (in a diocesan body or the Church Commissioners) on trusts which would give adequate powers of management and disposal.

Other church buildings used for parochial purposes but not belonging to the benefice, such as church halls and youth centres, are usually held by diocesan boards of finance and managed by parochial church councils.[2] Sometimes the buildings are held and managed by private trustees. In either case powers of management and disposal depend on the terms of the trust and on the general law governing charities and charitable trusts, and so present no special problem of church law.

The recent Sharing of Church Buildings Act 1969 enables the Church of England and other Churches to enter into agreements, which would operate as trusts, for the sharing or joint ownership of places of worship, church halls, residences and other buildings. The Act was necessary to overcome difficulties arising from the ecclesiastical law applying to Church of England churches and parsonage houses and from the trusts applicable to other Church of England buildings and the buildings of other Churches. An Act of Parliament was needed (instead of a Church Assembly Measure) because of its application to other Churches. Its terms illustrate the fact that legal complications involving statutory legislation are not confined to the Church of England.

CONCLUSION

The suggestions contained in this chapter require further detailed consideration. We hope that a proposal for a permanent Commission

---

[1]Some twenty Acts give powers of disposal, including the Ecclesiastical Leases Acts; the Ecclesiastical Leasing Acts; the Glebe Exchange Acts; the Glebe Lands Acts; the Parsonage Measure 1938; the Church Property (Miscellaneous Provisions) Measure 1960.
On dilapidations, the main legislation now in operation is the Ecclesiastical Dilapidations Measure 1923. Its complicated provisions are likely to be replaced soon by a new Measure which will put obligations to repair parsonage houses on diocesan bodies, and will simplify the obligations of incumbents in respect of glebe. This will improve matters, and some of the detail will be contained in schemes made by diocesan synods and approved by the Church Commissioners.
[2]See section 6 of the Parochial Church Councils (Powers) Measure 1956.

on church legislation, both Measures and Canons, will be considered by the General Synod. We think that a programme of consolidation and revision should be undertaken, and that its object should be not only to simplify and reduce the bulk of existing legislation, but also to avoid as far as possible the eventual need for legislation by Measure. We hope that our first exploration of the subject will be of use for this purpose.

183 There is a final point of importance. A programme of law revision which goes beyond pure consolidation, as this obviously must do, cannot make much progress unless a procedure is devised which avoids throwing open to debate the whole subject of a revising Measure, which may comprise much existing law. Parliament has a procedure of this kind for consolidation Bills, which may contain some amendments of a minor character, and also for the Bills of the Law Commission; and a similar procedure is sometimes applied to revising Bills which contain substantial changes of the law. The need for such a procedure is still greater in the General Synod with its limited time for legislative business. The procedure involves (1) entrusting a strong representative committee with the task of 'vetting' a revision Measure and reporting to the Synod on any provisions which seem to go beyond the objects of revision as laid down, and (2) limiting debate in the Synod to those provisions. The procedure can only work if all parties behave with maximum good faith and discipline.

We recommend the General Synod to undertake a programme of law revision, with the objects suggested in this chapter.

CHAPTER 6

Other Matters

MEMBERSHIP OF THE HOUSE OF COMMONS

Clergymen of the Church of England and ministers of the Church of Scotland are debarred from sitting in the House of Commons. A Roman Catholic in holy orders is likewise debarred.[1] A clergyman of the Church of England may resign his orders and so be eligible. A minister of the Church of Scotland may with the consent of the General Assembly relinquish his status as minister and so be eligible.

About this there are oddities. What principle is involved? It is not that clergy of a Church which has bishops in the House of Lords are debarred from the Commons because of these bishops; for the Roman Catholics have no bishops in the House of Lords and yet are debarred. Nor is it that clergy of a Protestant Church which has bishops in the House of Lords are debarred from the Commons because of these bishops; for the Macmanaway Case[2] showed that clergy of the Church of Ireland are disqualified, and the bishops of the Church of Ireland were ejected from the House of Lords a hundred years ago. Nor is it that a clergyman not a bishop is thought unfit to sit in Parliament. For a clergyman who may not sit in the Commons may sit in the Lords, provided he be an hereditary peer or a life peer.

The situation is less than logical.

Some of us would like to leave these laws unchanged. We argue thus. It has never been the genius of the Church of England to regard tidiness as the first of constitutional virtues. No one suffers an injustice by these Acts, since no one is prevented from being a candidate for Parliament if he wishes. In modern conditions a candidate for the House of Commons must stand as a member of a party. And if we are to choose between non-party bishops in the House of Lords and party priests in the House of Commons, we unhesitatingly choose the former. We suspect that this choice would need to be made if the repeal of these Acts were proposed.

We think that justice requires the repeal of the Act which debars Roman Catholic priests. They are in the same situation as Free Church Ministers who are not debarred by any Act. We think that justice requires the repeal of the Act so far as it affects clergymen in the Church

---

[1]House of Commons (Clergy Disqualification) Act 1801; Roman Catholic Relief Act 1829, Section 9.
[2]Privy Council report, Cmd 8067.

of Ireland, who are represented in the House of Lords by no bishops. And if justice requires so much, it ought also to allow clergy of the Church of England and ministers of the Church of Scotland the right to stand for Parliament. Indeed we can hardly imagine Parliament passing a Bill to remove two of the disabilities without removing them all. We prefer to think of them less as disabilities to the clergy, than as disabilities to Members of Parliament. Our age has seen the development of useful part-time or auxiliary ministries. Some men in business or the professions are also clergymen and remain in their business or profession. Why should a Member of Parliament, who thinks himself called to and qualified for a part-time ministry in the Church of England be prevented from being ordained?

We recommend that at a suitable opportunity the relevant clauses of the Acts be repealed.

PRIVILEGED COMMUNICATIONS

188   'The seal of the confessional' is a matter which in law is taken up into the wider heading of 'privileged communications', whether to clergymen, doctors, lawyers, or others who might receive in their professional capacity a statement which is made to them because the person stating it believes that as clergymen or doctors or lawyers they are under their professional honour and a binding obligation not to make public what they have thus heard privately.

189   The existence of this code of honour is quite as important to clergy as to doctors. It is of the first importance to their pastoral work that it should be known that a confidential communication is safe with them, indeed that they regard its secrecy as a sacred duty. Hence the need for some public statement of the fact: partly as a statement to the clergy of their obligation, and partly as a reminder to their people that such obligation exists.

190   The public statement now in force is contained in Canon 113 of the Canons of 1604. 'If any man confess his secret and hidden sins to the minister, for the unburdening of his conscience, and to receive spiritual consolation and ease of mind from him; we do straightly charge and admonish [the said minister], that he do not at any time reveal and make known to any person whatsoever any crime or offence so committed to his trust and secrecy (except they be such crimes as by the laws of this realm his own life may be called into question for concealing the same) under pain of irregularity'.

191   In 1947 the Convocations undertook to revise the Canons, and at first proposed in substance to re-enact the above, with the omission of the clause that the obligation ceased where the minister's life was in question. But such a re-enactment might be held to run contrary to the laws of England, where a person who refuses to give evidence when

required to do so in a court of law might be held to be guilty of contempt of court and punished.

Therefore the Convocations omitted any Canon on the subject for the time being.

Meanwhile the question of privileged communications came before the Law Reform Committee and the Criminal Law Revision Committee, who consulted the leaders of the Churches. The Archbishop of Canterbury produced evidence that in some other countries privileged communications to the clergy were safeguarded in the sense that they could not be compelled by a court of law to disclose them.

These committees did not recommend any change in the law. And at this point the Church of England Canon Law Standing Commission referred the difficulty to this Commission, as a problem which concerned the relations between Church and State.

The Law Reform Committee, in its Sixteenth Report (paragraph 46) argued that the point was academic rather than real. 'So far as we know, in the whole history of English law there never has been a civil case in which a minister of religion has been required to disclose a confession of sinful conduct made to him in his capacity as such minister in the exercise of his spiritual duties . . . so far as the law of evidence in civil cases is concerned, the problem appears to be without practical importance'.

The Law Reform Committee saw the difficulty in which it placed the Canons of the Church of England. But they felt a much greater difficulty in trying to draw a statutory distinction between such kinds of privileged communication in religion and other kinds, which would need to apply to all forms of religious denomination, even to those without a regular ministry. They preferred to rely on the wide discretion of judges rather than upon any statutory definition; and especially when (as they believed) such a case had not happened in England and (as they believed) was never likely to happen.

They made the same recommendations, as to judges' discretion, in the case of doctors.

The difficulty is constitutional in this way. The duty to keep religious confidences is a necessary part of the work of the Christian minister. It is an especial, indeed an exceptionally solemn, duty where the confidence is communicated as a private confession. Since the existence of this duty is so important to a pastoral ministry, the Church of England wishes to declare its existence in the most solemn manner possible. The natural way to make such a solemn declaration is to incorporate the duty in a Canon; especially as the duty is already incorporated in an existing Canon. Yet the Church of England cannot make a Canon which is contrary to the law of the land.

This situation is not peculiar to a Church whose links with the State are those of the Church of England. If a 'free Church' attempted to declare a binding rule of such a kind which was contrary to the law, that rule would be held invalid in the courts.

195 We have considered the possibility of a solemn or synodical declaration. The Convocation of Canterbury (but not the Convocation of York) passed such a declaration in 1959. It would be possible for the General Synod to re-affirm such a synodical declaration, as a statement not of the law but of the moral duty of Christian ministers.

196 The Law Reform Committee (paragraph 47 of its Sixteenth Report) though it did not recommend any change of statute, did envisage that such a change was not impossible. We are informed that in two jurisdictions of Canada, and in more than two-thirds of the jurisdictions of the United States, the privilege has been sanctioned by statute.[1]

197 For example, in Michigan and New York it is ruled: 'No minister of the Gospel, and no priest of any denomination whatsoever, shall be allowed to disclose any confessions made to him in his professional character, in the course of discipline enforced by the rules or practice of such denomination'.

198 We take the point of the Law Reform Committee that the matter is (we hope as they do) academic. We take also the point that it is the law's first and overriding duty to secure the proper administration of justice and that any sanction of a refusal to give evidence looks as though it is trying to put some other duty as a higher duty than justice. Nevertheless the duty laid upon a clergyman to observe the seal of the confessional is regarded as axiomatic. There are many other situations in which those concerned would regard themselves as under the same sort of restriction. We trust, therefore, the law will continue to be administered in such a way as not to require the revelation of confidences of this kind.

199 Since this matter was referred to the Commission, the situation has been altered to the extent that in the repeal of the Canons of 1603 that accompanied the promulgation of the new Canons of 1964 and 1969, the proviso to Canon 113 of the Canons 1603 was not included. The proviso still stands as part of the Constitutions and Canons Ecclesiastical of the Church of England. We think that the matter of privileged communications should now be left to rest, as it has in fact chiefly rested in the past, and must rest in the future, whether there is any further legislation by Canon or not, on the sense of moral obligation and pastoral responsibility.

---

[1]Wigmore's Treatise on the American Law of Evidence, Section 2395.

The law of marriage is not certain. It appears probable, that if the other conditions of the marriage are fulfilled, any two citizens of the country can claim to be married in their parish church and the incumbent has no right to refuse to marry them. This dates from the period when the only legal marriages, except for Quakers and Jews, were those celebrated in parish churches, and when except for Quakers and Jews almost everyone was baptised by Christian rites. But (in theory) a minister could probably be compelled to celebrate the marriage of two unbaptised persons.

This oddity has been referred to your Commission by the two Convocations at a session of 10th October 1966.

The Canon Law Commission of 1947 introduced a draft Canon which forbade the marriage in church of two unbaptised persons, and reserved to the bishop's discretion the cases where one of the two parties was not baptised. The Convocations and the House of Laity approved the draft Canon virtually without opposition. If one opinion of the law of England is correct, the Canon could not be implemented without the approval of Parliament.

The point has been declared to be 'largely academic'. Certainly we cannot imagine two persons, both of whom are unable to accept baptism, suing a minister because he felt himself unable to marry them.

We doubt whether the proposed Canon is in the best interests of the Church. Its real effect is less to remove from the unbaptised the right to be married in church than to remove from the parish minister the right to marry such persons at his pastoral discretion. Even from the debate which referred this question to us, it is clear that some ministers would regret the removal of their discretion. In that debate a speaker quoted the instance of members of the Salvation Army. Certainly it would make an odd Canon which on the one hand refused all discretion to the minister to consider the case of two persons who wholly accepted the Christian view of marriage but (perhaps by the accident of upbringing) have not been baptised, while on the other hand it compelled him to marry two persons who repudiated the Christian view of marriage but happened (perhaps by the accident of upbringing) to have been baptised as infants.

But although the proposed Canon is open to these objections, we consider some change in the law is desirable. It would be repugnant to large sections of Anglican opinion if marriages, where both parties were unbaptised, must by law be solemnised according to the rites of the Church of England, if the parties so desired. For at every turn the marriage service assumes that the parties are, by baptism, members of Christ's body. We believe the best way to deal with the matter would be to place the solemnisation of such marriages at the discretion of the minister guided by such regulations as may be made from time to time by the General Synod. He should not, by law, be compelled to solemnise such a marriage, but he should not, by law, be prevented from doing so, if he considers it warranted by the pastoral situation of the parties concerned. Parliament would be asked to adopt the same policy in regard to marriages in church where both parties are unbaptised, as it has already adopted in regard to marriages in church of those whose previous marriage has been dissolved and whose previous spouse is still living. In the adjustments of the relationship between Church and State, which our report proposes, we are of the opinion that the question of marriages in church, where both parties are unbaptised, should not be overlooked.

205 Nevertheless, though we hope that the General Synod will not enact the particular Canon which is proposed, we believe that this is essentially a spiritual matter, and the General Synod should have the right to pass such a Canon if on mature reflection it considers it to be the Christian course of action. The State has an interest in the solemnity of marriage, and to that extent has an interest in the work which the Churches perform in celebrating marriages. But the question whether a man and a woman are such that a Church may properly solemnise their marriage is one which their Church should determine. It can hardly be the State's interest to encourage those who do not accept the Christian view of marriage to use forms of words which make them profess publicly a view of marriage which they do not accept.

206 This question of the discipline of baptism touches another such question, which you have not referred explicitly to this Commission, but which is so parallel that it seems to go hand in hand. The minister has a legal obligation to baptise any baby which is brought to him by a parishioner. This dates from the time when the baptism was also (in effect) the civil registration. And on first sight the Church ought to hesitate before encouraging a minister to baptise a baby whose parents have every intention of not bringing him up in the Christian way and whose intention in bringing him to baptism is therefore in doubt. The modern State has no interest in such a question.

207 Such a law was in origin undoubtedly a law of the Church, and only became a law of the State because it was a law of the Church. A rule made for a time when nearly everyone had the intention of bringing up their children as Christians needs change in an age when not everyone has this intention.

208 The administration of baptism, and its consequences so far as they concern marriage or funerals,[1] are spiritual matters which should rightly be determined by the authorities of the Church of England.

---

[1] At present the law forbids the funeral service to be used for those who die unbaptised.

Into the enabling Measure which we propose – that is, the Measure which under safeguards permits the General Synod to determine the prayers of the Church of England – it would be possible to insert a clause giving the General Synod similar powers over the administration of baptism and its consequences for marriage and funerals.

Nevertheless we recognise that the problems of marriage and baptism cannot be solved in terms of rules and rights, but in the setting of pastoral care.

CHAPTER 7

Summary

RECOMMENDATIONS

211 (1) All matters affecting the worship and doctrine of the Church should
become subject to the final authority of the General Synod, with
certain safeguards provided.

(2) To this end, a Measure should be promoted to ensure that the
authority to order forms of worship already granted in part by
Parliament should be granted finally to the General Synod, under
certain safeguards (69, 77 and 86; and see Draft Measure in Appendix B).

(3) The same Measure should empower the General Synod to prescribe by Canon the forms of subscription to the doctrine of the
Church, and to interpret by Canon the formularies of the Church.
(83)

(4) A Committee or Electoral Board, representing both the diocese
concerned and the Church at large, should be formed to present the
Church's view when a bishop is to be nominated for election.
    We are not agreed on how such a Committee or Board should take
its place in the constitution of the Church.

   (*a*) Some of us recommend that the Committee should advise the
   Crown on the names of persons, through the Prime Minister. (114)

   (*b*) Some of us recommend the part of the Prime Minister should
   cease, and that the Electoral Board should elect the bishop, and
   present his name directly to the Sovereign. (131)

(5) The choice of suffragan bishops should be brought under the
system proposed in either (*a*) or (*b*) above, with the proviso that no
one should be chosen as suffragan without the consent of the diocesan bishop. (139)

(6) Leading members of other Communions, besides the bishops of
the Church of England, should be invited to sit in the House of Lords.
(155)

(7) No one should be excluded, by reason of being a minister of any
Church, from his right to stand as a candidate for Parliament and
to take his seat in the House of Commons. (187)

(8) Even in matters concerning church property the General Synod,
in its legislation, should be critical of any proposed Measure which

will necessarily lead in time to further Measures. It should be the eventual aim of the Synod to restrict Measures to fundamental changes of constitution or laws of property which affect secular rights, and to avoid all Measures which touch minor matters or matters where the intervention of Parliament is manifestly unnecessary (161; cf. creation or abolition of dioceses 166; residence of ministers, institutions, etc., 174; pensions, 176; parsonage houses and dilapidations, 179).

(9) To this end, the General Synod should undertake a programme of legislative consolidation and revision. (183)

CONCLUSION

In view of these recommendations, it may be asked, what would be left of 'establishment'? We are not much moved by this question, noticing that when church rates were abolished in 1868, or when the Local Government Act became law in 1894, or when the Enabling Act became law in 1919 (and doubtless on several other occasions), some said that it was equivalent to 'disestablishment'. If we persuade men to get away from loose general terms and consider actual laws, we shall have done a part of what we should like to do.

We think that a significant proportion of thinking people in this country would accept the proposition that the Church of England ought to stand further apart from the State than it now does. They would accept this for all sorts of different reasons, and what they mean by it would vary very much. But we have little doubt of that much widespread and basic agreement, though we are the last people to suppose that there would be unanimity on the question.

If this is so, there are obviously two possible destinations; (1) a total severing of the historic links, as in Ireland a hundred years ago and Wales fifty years ago; or (2) a form of legal polity resembling that which prevails in Scotland.

We have not recommended a total severing of the historic links; first, because we think such a programme to be impracticable in the present state of opinion; and second, because even if such a programme was practicable, most of us would not like it, though we should not shrink from it if the State decided it to be either wise or politically necessary. The people of this country value various features of our polity, and will not favour too much tampering. The people of England still want to feel that religion has a place in the land to which they can turn on the too rare occasions when they think that they need it; and they are not likely to be pleased by legislation which might suggest that the English people as a whole were going unChristian.

We have considered a Scottish solution, and reprint in Appendix E a part of what was written for the Howick Commission. What we recommend bears a distant resemblance to the Scottish Establishment. But we have not recommended an imitation of Scotland, because the circumstances which we meet are different from the circumstances of Scotland. The history of Church and State in the two countries has been very unlike since the Reformation if not before. We cannot take a system of law which has arisen in another part of Britain and impose it on England as though it fitted the facts, or the memories, of English life. We have to take English ecclesiastical polity as we find it and then see how it can be adapted.

217   Some people like England to have 'an established Church'. These persons value it for England's sake, less for the Church of England's sake. They think that the Christian tradition and the English inheritance go hand in hand. They do not want changes which end, or which jeopardise, a national recognition of religion, even if such a recognition can often be declared to be symbolic. They do not see how such a national recognition can continue if men make far-reaching proposals for change in the structure of what exists. They have little desire to extend the liberties of the Church, for they believe that the Church has already the liberties which it needs, in teaching, in choice of men, in worship, and in pastoral care.

218   Some people think the words 'established Church' to be an anachronism. Not that it is empty of meaning. But they find it used by different people with different meanings. They see a body of ecclesiastical laws, and ask which laws need altering, and, if they need altering, why? But they do not want to end a national recognition of religion. They want to adapt and amend the laws, so that the recognition may be wider, and less exclusive, and more ecumenical. They are deeply concerned, also, for what they see as the proper liberty of the Church in the things which concern its highest interests in worship or pastoral care or choice of men. One or two features of the law inherited from the past they tend to regard as fetters. They vary between feeling these fetters to chafe intolerably, and finding them comfortable now that we have been used to them for so long.

219   Some people think that 'an established Church' is bad. The State is secular, and the Church will do best not to be linked with it except as all voluntary bodies need its protection. These persons also are concerned for what they regard as the proper liberties of the Church. But even if the Church gained every liberty within a special nexus of law, as in Scotland, they would still think it bad. Only so, they think, will justice to a mixed population be seen to be done. Only so will the layers of the past be stripped away and reality prevail. Thus they have adopted the principles of the Independents in the age of the Reformation, that Church and magistrate must be sundered; forced thereto not by the religious axioms of the Independents, but by the plural nature of modern society.

In the light of such differences of approach, we have tried to recommend what the majority of us think to be desirable and practicable in what we judge (so far as we are able) to be the present state of the public mind.

The Church should concern itself first, and indeed second, with the poor and needy, whether in spirit or in body. We have been conscious that the first task of a Church is to look outwards, and that you have required us to look inwards, upon the constitution of the Church of England. We have steadily tried to remember that a constitution is not designed for the sake of a constitution. By lapse of years, or by change of human society, all systems of law must sooner or later be adjusted or become outmoded. We have recommended those adjustments which we think to be good in present circumstances. But we have tried to remember that gospel, sacraments, charity do not become outmoded and that these are the things that matter finally.

Memorandum of Dissent

By Miss Valerie Pitt

I

1 The Commission makes recommendations which, if accepted, would certainly modify the relations of the Church of England and the State in ways which are, at least in intention, fundamental. Their effect would be to deliver the secular government from inherited responsibilities peripheral to the running of a modern state, and the Church from the control which secular government still exercises over the manner of its worship and the intimacies of its pastoral care. Like most of my colleagues, and for much the same reasons, I believe that this deliverance is necessary for the welfare of the Church. Institutions, whether secular or religious, are like human beings; they are psychologically and spiritually handicapped if they do not carry responsibility for their own actions. The Church has long ago reached voting age: it is time it had the key of its own door.

Now as I am in so cordial an agreement with my colleagues it might seem mere eccentricity to trouble the Synods with dissent. I do so for three reasons:

2 Although the Commission genuinely intends to devolve responsibility from the State to the Church it preserves intact the legal apparatus of Establishment, and so leaves the State with a real, though no doubt formally exercised power, in the Church's affairs. This is impracticable: it preserves and breeds anomalies and brings the success of the Commission's proposals into question.

3 The Commission's attempt to conserve the historic forms of the Church/Crown relationship in England springs from assumptions about the Church, the constitution and the community which I do not share. It is, of course, possible to sign a report without committing oneself to every stage of its argument if its recommendations deserve the support of unanimity. I had considered that but the differences between myself and the Commission touch the quick of the Christian life. They ought not to be evaded.

4 The Commission's consensus on these questions represents a conventional Church of England wisdom. But there is another tradition in our Church's history. All Church and State Commissions, including this one, pay uneasy respect to the consciences of those who argue for the absolute claim of Christ to the allegiance of his Church. All Church and State Commissions, including this one, return rapidly to the claims

of history. So it is the case that the more radical of our traditions has never been stated in an official report except by people who were rejecting it. Unlike my colleagues, I do not believe that this strain has weakened in the Church. It is differently articulated: in an impatience with institutions and attitudes rather than in grand theological discussions about authority. It is often not very prudently expressed – but then prudence is not everything. It is there, it is deeply felt: it would be wrong if no one were to speak for it.

II

The Commission finds it can attach no exact meaning to the word establishment and is altogether uneasy about defining the phenomenon itself. Perhaps rightly: Establishment discussion about the Establishment tends to dwell on the 'givenness of English life' as though the Elizabethan settlement were a platonic entity, an idea laid up in the mind of God. This confusion is better avoided. Yet the Commission exaggerates the difficulty. The legal relations of the Church of England with the State are complex, often tangled and irrational: they are not obscure. The questions about which the Commission is most concerned, the control of doctrine and worship, the control of pastoral discipline, the appointment of bishops, are now regulated by the statutory arrangements made in the sixteenth century both to assert and to ensure the Royal Supremacy.[1] Of course, the apparatus of Church life was there to the Tudor hand. Henry VIII did not invent dioceses, parishes, Lords Spiritual or Church courts, but then these are not the Establishment: they are subsumed in it. Establishment in England, so far as it is a practical reality and not a nostalgia or a cock-shy, is a legal edifice resting on twin Tudor pillars: the King's power and right to direct and oversee the Church's life; the subject's obligation to attend and maintain the Church 'by law established'.

Most of all this is embodied in and has been extended or modified by statute. Of course it does not work quite as the Tudors intended: neither Henry VIII nor the first Elizabeth had had the advantage of reading Burke or Bagehot; they were innocent of any doctrine of constitutional monarchy, certainly of popular democracy. For them and their immediate successors the Royal Supremacy was personal, not the exercise of a popular will mysteriously embodied in the Sovereign but the Sovereign's own power and right. The elaborate machinery of parliamentary debate and ministerial consultation, the advice of the Prime Minister and the patronage of the patronage secretary formed no part of the settlement of religion: they belong to the long process of constitutional development by which the powers of the Sovereign were

---

[1]See Appendix A.

devolved into the hands of Ministers responsible to an elected House of Commons. Although the Queen is, like the first Elizabeth, Supreme Governor of the Church of England, it would be constitutionally improper for her to promote decrees about Church affairs or to nominate, directly, to the episcopate.

7 The Commission's proposals bypass this constitutional commonplace. They assume that the Supremacy is still, in some ways, personal to the Sovereign; that it can be set apart from the other jurisdictions of the Crown and exercised if not directly by the Sovereign at least by the Sovereign in concert with the Church itself. This is not so much of an innovation as it sounds: even now, it is the diocesan bishop who proposes names for his suffragans; he is not obliged to consult with the Prime Minister or the patronage secretary. Again, the Commission's recommendations on doctrine and worship adapt the procedures used in the recent revision of Canon Law which received the Royal Assent without the intervention of Parliament. This obviously involved a direct exercise of the Supremacy (under the Act for the Submission of the Clergy) though probably by historical accident. As the code of Canons has not been revised since the early seventeenth century, the procedures for promulging them remained pristine and anomalous, uneroded by three centuries of constitutional development. Yet the procedures, however anomalous exist. The structures of government themselves permit a more sensible and flexible exercise of the Supremacy and one which can be more aligned with the decisions of the Church. This is at any rate the Commission's common faith, the *sine qua non* of its recommendations. The more conservative of its members acquiesce, perhaps, in such a realignment because it leaves the edifice of Establishment standing and untouched, the more radical hope for it because it represents a real shift of power within the existing system and, what is more, a shift which will acquire a momentum so that, in time, the Church will gently and without any major upheaval, coast into its freedom. This, I think, may well turn out to be an illusion.

8 It is a very plausible illusion. It is indeed likely that, once the Commission's proposals were accepted, the State's role in the Church's affairs would be increasingly governed by convention. The secular government has, as government, no serious interest in the doctrine and discipline of the Church and therefore, no interest in actively interfering with or overriding its common decisions even supposing that it had time to spare from its own proper business. In normal practice then, the Crown's veto would not be exercised but so long as it exists it is possible for the State to use it. Indeed, this has happened and not only in 1928 and not only in Parliament. It is not irrelevant that two of the matters referred to this Commission arise from difficulties in the promulging of the Canon Law. Two Canons, that on the marriage of the unbaptised and that on the seal of the confessional were discreetly withdrawn from the code presented for the Royal Assent because it was intimated that

they were unlikely to get it. This does not suggest any inevitable smoothness for the procedures the Commission proposes for the control of doctrine and worship. Let us suppose that the Prayer Book of 1928 had not been presented to Parliament in a Church Assembly Measure but appended to a revised Canon and presented for the Royal Assent it seems improbable that the then Home Secretary would have advised the Sovereign to give it. There is nothing in the Commission's proposals to prevent a harassed or cautious Home Secretary from tendering the same advice when the Royal Assent is asked for the Prayer Book revisions of 1998.

A different but still a political difficulty arises about the appointment of bishops. We do not know whether the Sovereign's personal wishes are consulted about nominations to the Bench, but it is no historical secret that some very distinguished churchmen have not enjoyed the confidence of their respective monarchs. This did not, necessarily, make them unsuitable pastors for Christ's flock; and if the Prime Minister nominated such a man to a bishopric that, constitutionally, would settle the matter. But suppose the board proposed by the Commission should elect some future Dean Swift or Bishop Bell: it has and can have no power to compel a reluctant Sovereign to accept its choice, nor could it offer to use the Prime Minister as an intermediary. Indeed, the Prime Minister might himself be an obstacle; for whether the Church's nomination is made direct to the Sovereign or by convention, through the Prime Minister, it is clear that no Sovereign could appoint a bishop who, though chosen by the Church, was unacceptable to the government of the day at least, not while the Church remains established. Some members of the Commission might argue that under their proposals, for an *advisory* board the problem would never arise, partly because the board advises only, partly because the processes of consultation would themselves sieve out candidates known to be unacceptable to the Sovereign or his Ministers. And that, in the way of the world, is only too likely. Unfortunately it does not solve the problem, for in this situation the State's veto, though never actually exercised, would always be active in the system and moreover in that unopen, behind scenes way which, for many of us, is a morally detestable feature of the present arrangements. All this highlights the flaw in the Commission's proposals. Of course, it is possible to make the machinery of the Establishment work in ways which apparently advance the Church's freedom provided that the situation is normal. If it were difficult or ambiguous, the State's latent powers could be re-animated; only in the new arrangements they would work differently, less obtrusively and therefore more objectionably. It is one thing, after all, to have Parliament publicly rejecting Prayer Book proposals, quite another to have decisions about the Church's worship turn on a Home Office interpretation of a Canon. The Commission may be repeating the mistake the Church made at the time of the Enabling Act, that is, that it may be deluded into believing that its proposals would give the Church a freedom which could operate without the co-operation of government. The only difference is that whereas in 1927 and 1928 the mistake became publicly obvious, under these proposals, all such problems could be discreetly settled out of public earshot and question.

III

10 These risks are inherent in any attempt to maintain the relationship between the Crown and the Church – but why take them? Since we all desire freedom of action for the Church and the obstacle to that is where it has always been – in the terms of the Tudor settlement of religion – there seems to be a straight choice, 'Bondage with ease – or strenuous liberty', or at least between some administrative adjustment (which is what Howick proposed) and a more radical change not simply in the conventions which govern us but in the law itself. The Commission would reply that the history and present condition of our Church deny us the luxury of simple choices even if we could persuade each other to make them. We cannot now return to the *status quo ante* Howick, but neither can we treat the Tudor settlement as a thing apart. It has grown (or rusted) deep into the Church's life and its institutions. That is fair: what is required here is, precisely, a judgement; a decision stemming from the analysis and balance of all the elements in a complex situation. The members of the Commission have a variety of personal insights: they do not all give the same weight to the same considerations, but they have come to a common understanding that, at the present stage in the Church's history, we have to accept a less than ideal solution to the problems of its government. The Commission in a common mind is very impressive – but then its understanding of the situation is not mine.

11 What it believes is that the historic relationship of Church and people in England is still live, if only as a sentiment inhibiting change, in our society. The Englishman's traditional indifference or antipathy to the Church's institutions, his habitual neglect of its common worship is, though regrettable, irrelevant. Established religion, the parish church, bishops in the House of Lords, the Thirty-nine Articles, are so much his cultural context that, unless he explicitly opts out of membership and into another religion, he is, he must be, deep down C. of E. Indeed he says he is to pollsters and on the appropriate forms. The fact that he also expresses views totally at variance with any form of historic Christianity is a minor difficulty: what matters is the continuance and preservation of this 'folk religion'. The members of the Commission see it in various ways – as the aliveness of the Christian past in our less faithful present, as a true but inarticulate belief wickedly undervalued by sectarian intellectuals, and as a pastoral opportunity. Whatever it is, this cultural Anglicanism, the 'givenness' of Christianity in English life

would be deeply affected, they believe, by radical changes in legal Establishment, and especially by any alteration in the position of the Sovereign. For the relationship between Church and people is not so much represented as mysteriously achieved in the Crown. An extreme view, held both in the Commission and in the Church, is that the Sovereign herself embodies the people in its relationship with God, and safeguards the interests of millions of folk Anglicans against the activities of unrepresentative Synods. Even though one may be sceptical of such a view its existence makes it difficult to propose any changes which touch on the prerogatives of the Crown itself.

I am convinced that both of these propositions are mistaken and that the second, which underlies the Commission's deliberate adherence to the Supremacy, is constitutionally unfortunate. For England is not Byzantium. It is true that many people find the Sovereign a symbolic person, fewer perhaps a link between the nation and God, and the sentiment is if theologically doubtful, historically understandable. Yet as a principle of political action it simply ignores three hundred years of English history. In the constitutional present the Crown has no such divinity: its prerogatives poise the powers of the other organs of government – but then in the equilibrium of the state, all the elements of its order, Parliament, the courts, the electorate balance each other. Perhaps the most disturbing feature of the Commission's proposals and of some of its reasoning is their tendency to take traditional and symbolic appearances for present reality. The Sovereign does not personally agree to the Canons: Home Office lawyers do. She does not, and neither does the Prime Minister, engage personally in the choice of bishops: the Patronage Secretary does. Most of all, the Sovereign does not in a functional sense represent the people: the House of Commons does. If it were indeed true that the three-quarters of the population who ignore it altogether have a profound interest in the Church of England's affairs, that would be an argument, though not altogether a valid one, not for maintaining the Sovereign's part in the Church's government but for transferring her powers in it, formally, to Parliament.

But is it true? It would be surprising, or rather culturally impossible, if after so many centuries, the nation had taken no imprint in the forms of its life and its moral style from its association with the Church. Only unlike the Commission I am not persuaded that what remains of this C. of E. idiom in our way of life represents a lively faith in the gospel or even that it is, any longer, a pastoral opportunity or an effective sentiment outside the Church's own institutions. This is the crucial difference between myself and the Commission, and it is not so much a difference about the interpretation of statistics as of experience and theology. All of us readily admit that the strength of cultural Anglicanism is more evident in some areas and classes than it is in others, but for those of us who work and live in great conurbations, or among the young, the argument that the doings of the Church of England are central in the lives of our colleagues, our families and our acquaintances is just unreal. We do not know the folk who are so deeply concerned with the ordering of Anglican worship or the appointment of Anglican bishops. The encounter with the third generation of urban indifference, documented right back to the Victorian Church, gives a slightly different picture of the place of the Church in English life. In this a man who involves himself with the Church, who practises his faith does so not with but against the conventions of society and increasingly against the grain of his cultural inheritance. He is forced to make a choice and that, I believe, is no desperate ill. For in fact Christianity is not a folk or a tribal religion, it is not bred into us by the traditions of our ancestors. It is a gospel, a revealed religion, demanding an active and personal assent. To be a Christian a man must himself answer – *Jesus is Lord*. Writing 'C. of E.' on a form is not quite enough.

14 The traditional argument that the link between Church and Crown must be retained for historical and cultural reasons is no longer acceptable because our culture itself, as it grows away from its Christian roots, increasingly compels us to choose an allegiance. And there is some danger that if we persist in this argument we may deepen and confirm the Englishman's habitual confusion of the Faith with a culture. This confusion is most obvious when simple people, of all backgrounds, present the sometimes limited moral codes and attitudes of their class and generation as 'Christ's teaching' and then blame the Church for not proclaiming that in the name of God. The muddle is however more insidious in what, for want of a better term, we may call the metaphysical content of folk religion. The surveys which reveal a sixty odd per cent English claim to be C. of E. also show what we know from other sources that, for a good many people, Christianity is a comfortable mix of ancestral attitudes (everything from astrological superstition to yesterday's liberalism), inconsistent both with each other and with the historic gospel. It is certainly inconsistent with the Prayer Book formularies which the Commission is entrenching in its proposals for the control of doctrine and worship. To assert that this popular *Weltanschauung* is an 'implicit Christianity' to be carefully safeguarded by the maintenance of the forms of Establishment is to forget the distinctive claims of the gospel, especially, perhaps, our belief that it is revealed truth. What is more, this kind of folk religion, where it still exists, is often profoundly nostalgic: deeply entwined with childhood or with folk memories of life in small, close-knit local communities – ways of life now outside the experience of millions. We may find ourselves identifying faith not merely with culture but with a dying culture.

15 The Commission's most deeply felt and most eloquent arguments are touched with this nostalgia. Of course no Christian can undervalue

history since history is the medium of our redemption. Of the Church's past alive in the nation's present it is possible to say without blasphemy that it is 'The footsteps of His life in mine'. And having said that we have also to say that history is history: our encounter with Christ is always *now*. The institutions of the Christian past are venerable, beautiful, hallowed in our own experience but what of that? When the shape, the structure, the colour of English life is changing what we have to ask is are they apt to present Christ to generations impatient of the appeal to tradition?

IV

All this makes me believe that the Church not only can but ought to make a straight choice, virtually between the past and the future. If it cannot bring itself to do so I would support the Commission's proposals: half a step in the right direction is better than standing still. The Commission's intentions, however, will be more fully achieved if the Church goes a step further. *I propose therefore that the Church should ask the State to take whatever action is necessary to repeal or render ineffective these statutes and any other legislation consequent on or reinforcing their provisions:*

(1) *The Submission of the Clergy Act 1533*, which deals with the Royal Assent to Canons.
(2) *The Appointment of Bishops Act 1533, the Suffragan Bishops Act 1534 and the Suffragans Nomination Act 1888.*
(3) *The Act of Supremacy of 1558 and the Clerical Subscription Act 1865.*
(4) *The Acts of Uniformity.*

This is a proposal to dismantle the legal apparatus of the Royal Supremacy so as to give the Church of England the status enjoyed by all other Churches in Great Britain except the Church of Scotland. But the Church of England is not, for historic reasons, quite as other Churches in Great Britain, and it might be thought proper, as a gesture to history and for other reasons, for the Sovereign to retain a special relationship with the Church of England not as Supreme Governor, for that necessarily commits the secular Government to a part in the Church's affairs, but as patron or guardian.

It would follow, as a matter of justice, that those provisions of the law, in the Act of Settlement and other Acts, which relate to the personal religion of the Sovereign and his family should be removed; but if the Sovereign were to become the guardian of the Church it would be necessary only to make the minimum of changes in the coronation oath: to omit, for instance, the words 'established by law' and the requirement to maintain the settlement of the Church of England, but not the promise to maintain the laws of God and the true provision of the gospel. The more delicate difficulties of that oath might then be left to be considered, when the time came, by a more ecumenical generation.

19 As the coronation itself forms no part of the Tudor settlement, proposals to dismantle that settlement raise no other question about it except this: Should the rite itself remain in an Anglican form? And this again is a question to be settled (if it is still relevant) at the time.

20 The coronation is only the most spectacular outcrop of our feudal sub-structure. There is also the odd personal and pre-establishment relationship which still subsists between the Crown and the bishops. The bishops pay homage to the Crown and sit in the House of Lords for the same medieval reason: their predecessors in office held feoffs of the King.

21 The continuing presence of the bishops in the House of Lords then depends on whether the nation wants its second chamber in the legislature to remain a feudal institution. If it wants it reformed then the Christian Churches have, as communities within the community a case but not a right to be represented there, though not necessarily by their bishops or bureaucrats. It is a matter for the State to decide and so is the question about whether elected bishops should remain members of an unreformed House of Lords.

22 The ceremony of episcopal homage is another matter. It should go and with it the obligation laid on beneficed Anglican clergymen to take oaths of allegiance to the Crown. There is no reason why a clergyman should be constrained to loyalty oaths not required of the ordinary citizen and in any case the whole business is unfitting and always has been. Christian ministers are lieges of Christ, the servants of peace, not the military vassals of a feudal Sovereign.

23 If these proposals were accepted the Church would need to provide for and give authority to its own forms of government. Fortunately, the structures of such government are already to its hand in the provisions of the Synodical Government Measure which it would need to reaffirm, possibly with some modifications as an Act of Synod, bearing its own authority rather than the combined authority of the Assembly and Parliament. I propose that in this changed situation the Synod should,
   1. *Re-enact, with any necessary modifications, the Synodical Government Measure.*
   2. *Accept the Commission's proposals for the control of worship and doctrine.*
   3. *Accept the second of the Commission's proposals for the election of bishops with the proviso that the bishop elect should be presented to his diocesan synod so that they may formally receive him as their father in God.*

24 There are certain other matters which would require more consideration. First, under these proposals the Church's disciplinary courts would cease to be courts of law. It would be for the Synods to consider whether their present composition and structure is best adapted to their new role.

Second there is a question about the position of the Church Commissioners, or rather, and more importantly, about the proper financial institutions for a Church independent of parliamentary control. The Church Commissioners come, in any case, within our terms of reference in two ways. First, they are, as a corporation, amphibian, created originally by Parliament to deal with the financial affairs of the Church and enjoying a dual membership of representatives both of the Church and of the State. Second, they have certain quasi-judicial functions, especially related to the territorial ministry of the Church, which derive ultimately from the mandate Parliament gave them. Their internal administration and the management of their capital were not our concern. The existence of that capital becomes, however, significant when we consider dissenting proposals. For the Commissioners manage most of the ancient endowments of the Church and it is argued (which is odd – since the Tudors did not exactly endow the Church) that any radical alteration in the terms of the Elizabethan settlement necessarily brings those endowments into question. It will because people expect it to, but, in the long run I think this argument a bogey. It is difficult to conceive of a modern government deliberately taking steps to impoverish the clergy because the Church asks to elect its own bishops and choose its own forms of prayer. It is equally difficult to agree with those who think that if we couldn't pay the clergy that would bring us into a spiritual revival. The question is more complex than that.

For we are not only concerned with the State's attitude to our endowments but with our own. It is now a question whether the Church can, given the limitation of its income from all sources, afford the expense of Establishment if Establishment implies the maintenance and support of our cultural and structural inheritance: the parochial system, the maintenance of great cathedrals and other historical buildings and the Church's educational and social work. Its difficulties are compounded by its own financial structures – the existence of two central bodies, the Commissioners which has a responsibility to the State, and the Central Board of Finance, which has not, would seem to be uneconomical as well as frustrating. Even if we made no progress at all with any of our other proposals, it would be right that the Church should give some attention to its financial institutions and responsibilities, and I therefore propose:

That the Church should ask the Government to join it in a review of the present structure and responsibilities of the Church Commissioners for England, and that such an enquiry should consider among other things ways and means of making the corporation more clearly and directly answerable to the General Synod of the Church of England.

For the powers which have accrued to the Commissioners in the development of their original mandate give them an influence in society which must make their near-autonomy a matter of concern both to the Church and to the State.

26 If the Church were to accept proposals for dismantling the Elizabethan settlement it would need to undertake a similar enquiry with a view to establishing new financial structures, and would have to enter into negotiations with the State about the position and capital of the Commissioners and about some of their traditional responsibilities.

V

27 All this, it will be objected, disestablishes the Church. Of course it does. The Commission's majority proposals do not: with one important exception they leave the enactments by which the Church was established entirely untouched. These proposals undo them. They do not, however, withdraw the Church from the national life or from its service to the community for these are not a matter of law or of legal status. A Church's national character:

> is a matter of how it understands its churchly calling, and does not depend for its reality on the status which the national community gives it.

That, surprisingly, is a quotation from the Report of the Anglican-Methodist Unity Commission and it will serve as a text. For although one is bound to argue a dissenting case negatively, as an objection to the majority proposals, I believe that there is a positive argument for the separation of Church and State though not of the Church from the community.

It is necessary, now, for the Church's realisation (that is, its awareness of and its making real) of its churchly calling. The fact of legal establishment has bred a profound contradiction between the Church of England's easy acceptance of its cultural position and its understanding of its nature and work in Christ. A body which prays 'The bread which we break, is it not a sharing of the Body of Christ?' and yet expects, not without complacency, that at least three-quarters of its nominal members (those entitled to elect to its councils) will never share in that broken bread has, surely, a divided mind and a divided will. These are not the best instruments to deal with a mission situation. We need to discover our identity in Christ, our coherence in him and we cannot do this, we are not doing it, in the conditions of historical establishment.

28 There is another side to this. There is a strong tendency in the Church of England to place far too heavy an emphasis on law and legal status, to find the essence and identity of the community not in common life but in structures and institutions. This is almost inevitable in a Church so dependent on a legal settlement, but it is disastrous at the present time. For what Henry VIII did amongst other things was to perpetuate in a less remote and therefore more intolerable form, the Roman centralisation of Church government. Hence the Church of England

passion for centralisation, uniformity, elaborate committee structures and central advisory bodies. Yet in a situation of rapid but uneven cultural and social change such a passion for structures and ways imposed from above is not only inappropriate but inevitably defeated. The identity and coherence of the Church will in the long run be discovered and realised in the *ecclesiae*, the local communities of Christians. What we desperately need now are ways and structures which will help to build those local and limited allegiances into the catholic order of the whole Body of Christ. In the present Church-State relationship this is impossible for it is itself a relationship between centralised authorities: the Crown, Parliament and the central institutions of the Church. These links have to be modified, broken, before the Church can in any way begin to release, or to feel within its structures the energies of its 'ordinary' congregations.

The important word is begin. Great changes take more than a generation (however fluid the cultural situation) to have their full effect, and it is not to be supposed that these or any other measures will transform the Church of England overnight. It is indeed because of the necessary slowness with which any reforming programme achieves its purpose that we cannot afford, in a reluctance to abandon the hallowed and the familiar, the luxury of half measures. For, after all, the future also has its history – us: it is not fair to build our nostalgias, still more our fathers' nostalgias, into our grandchildrens' lives.

VALERIE PITT

We are in broad agreement with the proposals made in the above Memorandum, but would like to add the following notes.

PETER CORNWALL
DENIS W. COE

ditional Note by Mr Cornwall

It is with deep regret that I am unable to sign the Commission's Report. I fully support those recommendations which seek to secure freedom for the Church to order its own worship and doctrine and to choose its own bishops. However, if the Church of England were to win these freedoms, it would still retain a special relationship to the State, similar in practise to that which exists in Scotland, and it is the peculiar status which arises from this relationship which I feel bound to question.

I believe that the national recognition of the Church of England gives it a privileged position which cannot be justified. It is true that our Church appears more privileged than in fact it is, but the status it acquires from its connection with the Crown and the representation it is given in the House of Lords, makes the question of privilege a live one. The Commission underestimates the offence which is caused, not only to critics of the Church but also to some of its loyal members, by the community of the Crucified Servant accepting too easily a privileged status. Moreover, at a time of turmoil and anguish within the Church, we are tempted to find our security in ancient privileges and institutions rather than in that Gospel upon which the authority and power of the Church alone depends. I believe that the Church should accept this stripping of privilege and prestige in order to communicate its Gospel to a generation which accepts no institution which appears to be kept in existence by the props of external authority.

3   I believe that the national recognition of the Church of England gives the impression that England is more Christian than it really is, and encourages delusions of grandeur within the Church itself. The sociological evidence shows that a very large number of English people wish to be thought of as C. of E. This evidence certainly forbids any sweeping theories about the secularisation of England and indicates that the Church is surrounded by a wide penumbra which is a mixture of nostalgia, superstition and genuine desire for faith. This puzzling phenomenon of diffused and inarticulate religion needs to be treated with pastoral sensitivity and discrimination, yet it must be distinguished from that definite ecclesiastical commitment without which it is impossible to justify the national recognition of an ecclesiastical institution. While we are never in a position to judge how near men are to the Kingdom of God, we are in a position to know how near they are to the visible institutional Church. Sunday by Sunday the registers of our parish churches tell this tale. I believe that the national recognition of the Church of England encourages people in the belief that Christianity is something you can inherit without personal decision and that rights of Church membership can be enjoyed without corresponding duties. The warm generosity of our Church towards the man who struggles for faith is one thing, and greatly to be commended, but that woolliness which offers false reassurance is another. There is a point where Anglican generosity becomes Anglican wool, and I fear that the notion of a national Church blurs this point. I believe also that the special status accorded to the Church inhibits us from accepting the truth that we are a minority group. We do not show Christian love by encouraging delusions in both Church and nation.

4   For these two reasons, that national recognition gives to the Church inappropriate privilege and dangerously masks realities, I believe that the Church should seek, not only those freedoms which the Commission has recommended, but to abandon that special status which it is accorded in the land. In particular I would recommend that the Church should indicate its willingness to cease to be represented by bishops in the House of Lords.

5   I confess that I almost lose my nerve at this point when I contemplate the misunderstandings and forebodings that such a recommendation

would arouse. Many believe that this would be the signal for the Church to opt out of the life of the nation and retire into a cosy if pious ghetto. Many too believe that the Church would sacrifice its broad inclusive character and become narrowly sectarian. If I believed that either of these consequences would follow from what I have argued then I would have chosen the problems of a national Church as the lesser of two evils. I am utterly committed both by theological conviction and pastoral experience to the view that the Church should be involved in the life of the nation and should retain its historic liberality and openness. I have therefore had to decide whether these valuable marks of the Church of England are in fact dependent upon the Church-State relationship. My conclusion has been that, whatever may have been true in the past, there is no such dependence now and that true national involvement and Anglican liberality are at present distorted by this relationship.

The involvement of the Church in the life of the nation does not depend upon any special status offered to the Church and its clergy, for the Church is wholly involved where its laity are involved. The man in the street may believe that the Church expresses its social concern when a bishop speaks out in the House of Lords, but in fact the Church expresses concern more deeply and effectively when Christian Members of Parliament wrestle with the problems of power in the House of Commons. The latter involvement may be harder for the world to see, but Christian witness in society does not depend upon advertisement. The special status of the Church of England encourages an official and clerical style of involvement, while the style which appears more appropriate to the servant Church is one which abandons special status, and on equal terms shares with others the problems of power in an anonymous and unadvertised way, winning authority only by professional competence and persuasiveness. The question at issue is not whether the Church should be involved in the life of the nation, but what form this involvement should take. I believe that our concern should be moved from the House of Lords to the House of Commons, from the role of senior clergy to the role of laity.

Nothing in my experience of the Church of England so far leads me to believe that its liberality and openness depend upon its special legal status. I would certainly argue that the parochial system, providing for a resident priest in every area who is free to develop a wide-ranging interest in the locality, does assist such openness. However the parochial system in no way depends upon the Church-State connection. Where this connexion does impinge upon the local situation and people are led to believe that they have rights to the ministrations of the Church, then I believe the wrong sort of inclusiveness is encouraged. If the Church of England is to be both realistic about its minority status and able to be a generous and sensitive minority, we shall have to discover the right sort of openness which does not pretend that religious aspirations and church membership are the same thing. The vocation to both holiness and catholicity is laid upon the Church. It must be holy, possessing that distinctive shape and form which arises, not from its ancient institutions, but from a community united in a common faith, and yet catholic, with a community so secure in faith that it can be alert and sensitive to the working of God outside its borders. Such inclusiveness does not spring from laws which make us pretend that every Englishman is C. of E. at heart or that one can be a Christian without decision and commitment, but from the conviction that the Lord of the Church also works outside his Church.

8 Attracted as I am by the considerable advances which I see in the Commission's recommendations, I am obliged to declare myself a reluctant disestablishmentarian. I declare myself so with reluctance because I have no illusions about the dangers of that narrow exclusive attitude which a small group can display, and because I shrink from turmoil in the Church of England over what is, on any count, a matter of secondary importance. I have felt it right to declare my attitude towards the national recognition of the Church of England because I believe that the time has come when certain institutional props need to be removed in order to help the Church rediscover its own identity and commend its faith without the aid of privileged status.

PETER CORNWELL

Additional Note by Mr Coe

1 When I joined the Commission my inclination was to believe that the necessary changes in the relationship between the Church of England and the State could be achieved by a modified form of establishment, and the more radical proposals which have been put forward by the Commission are in sympathy with such a belief. It therefore makes my regret at not being able to sign the main Report very great indeed.

2 But by highlighting the position of the Crown prerogative in her Memorandum of Dissent, Miss Pitt has pointed to a major difficulty in implementing the Commission's proposals. Unlike her I would not wish to stress the possibility of an open or public breach between Crown and Church; the conventions of constitutional monarchy would in my view make such a clash impossible. For the Crown to take an independent line in this way, accompanied by the inevitable controversy, would surely invite the early demise of the monarchy as we know it, and rightly so. Obviously then, in any constitutional changes which are proposed, the Crown must be safeguarded from the possibility of expressing a sectional interest. If the Queen is expected to give approval to any particular action, however formally, it must always be done on the advice of her Ministers so that the responsibility for such an action is clearly established.

There is also force in the argument that if the Queen's assent is retained in such matters as Canon Law there could be difficulties of interpretation between the established Church and the Crown's advisers, resulting in the matter being discreetly dropped before it ever reached the Queen. As the Memorandum of Dissent has pointed out, this would perpetuate one of the worst aspects of the present arrangements.

It is for these reasons that I consider it would be bad constitutional practice to suggest the removal of Her Majesty's Ministers from matters concerning the relationship between the established Church and State, if it is considered necessary to retain the need for the Queen's assent.

The Church of England must really make up its mind on whether it wants a completely free hand in such matters as appointments and worship. If it does then the assent of the Crown ought to be ended.

Apart from the position of the Crown, the main Report has drawn attention to the difficulty which may arise over the right of bishops to sit in the House of Lords if the role of the Prime Minister in their appointment to a bishopric were to be abolished. At the present stage of British constitutional development I believe that a second chamber of Parliament is necessary. I would end the right of hereditary peers to sit in the House of Lords and would abolish its delaying power. This would create a useful second chamber which would be able to initiate and revise legislation and act as a form of debate. In such a reformed second chamber I am not convinced that either law lords or bishops need to sit as of right. The recent White Paper on the reform of the House of Lords suggested that the Prime Minister's appointments to the life peerage should be scrutinised by a committee to see that a fair balance of interests were represented. It would seem to me reasonable that in a reformed House of Lords, without a specific quota of judges and bishops, appointments to the life peerage would include some who were prominent in Church circles and could include both bishops from the Church of England and leading churchmen from other denominations.

In addition to these constitutional issues I am concerned about the ecumenical aspect of our work. In our terms of reference the Commission was charged, 'to take account of current and future steps to promote greater unity between the Churches'. Throughout our discussions I have supported the more radical approach contained in the main Report but, as the final picture of our proposals has emerged, I have an uncomfortable feeling that we want to retain a privileged position in relation to our fellow Christians in other denominations. If this is so then we will surely hamper greater unity between the Churches rather than promote it.

Finally, like my two colleagues who also dissent from the Report, I question the claim for universality which is made by the Established Church. I believe that, far from being universal, there is a danger that for social, political and economic reasons the Church of England still gives the appearance of being closely associated with the middle and upper classes and therefore, in a practical sense, seems rather exclusive. Certainly a high proportion of the population covering all classes choose to identify themselves as being members of the Church of England but, for the reasons I have mentioned, many seem to gain little from such an identification.

8 During the last four years, then, I have moved from my original position and have come to feel that these constitutional, ecumenical and social considerations make disestablishment a right step to take. It will not bring about any dramatic changes but it will enable the Church of England to re-examine its mission and strategy and it will be seen to have full control over and responsibility for the ordering of its affairs.

DENIS W. COE

Note of Dissent (to Chapter 2 only)

By Sir Timothy Hoare

I do not consider it wise to attempt now a complete transfer from the Crown in Parliament to the General Synod of the final authority in matters of doctrine and worship.

Parliament, of course, has the sovereign power to pass any Act it chooses, relating to the Church or anything else in Britain. In the terms of the Enabling Act, however, it has no right to amend Church Measures. It has only a power of veto and this has been exercised on only one matter of substance. With this situation I am generally content but I recognise that the strength of opinion against the present affirmative resolution procedure and some alleged awkwardness in its administration makes a change desirable. The Commission's solution is surgical and final. Because I believe the system has an intrinsic value as well as being a meaningful symbol of the partnership of Church and State (that is to say of Church and nation), which an Established Church implies, I have ventured to suggest an alternative modification of the present procedure.

There would be advantages for the Church in a modification rather than the abolition of the present system. The Church is in the process of trying to establish a new form of government in which it is hoped that there will be full representation of the laity. For some years yet this will be untried and in the nature of an experiment. It may not be right to jettison the whole of the old pattern before the new has established its effectiveness. Paragraph 67 expresses the hope that the General Synod will be fully representative of the lay members of the Church of England. Unfortunately, constitutions do not always achieve what they set out to do. A judgement on the success of Synodical Government on this matter will not be possible for at least ten years. High hopes were expressed at the time of the creation of the Church Assembly about the representative quality of its lay membership. Lord Selborne, whose Commission was responsible for setting in motion the Enabling Bill, himself admitted later that these hopes were not fulfilled. At no time since 1930 have the electoral rolls included more than 41 per cent of the confirmed or 16 per cent of the baptised members of the Church. Recent members on the rolls (1968) are about a third below these peaks, that is to say, 27 per cent of the confirmed or 9·5 per cent of the baptised. Only a dramatic increase in the number of those signing the rolls can give the Synod an electorate comparable with the wider membership of the Church.

4   Paragraphs 102–104 justify the part played by the Crown in the appointment of bishops on the grounds that the Church's organs of government do not always prove to be fully representative. I submit that this argument is also valid in relation to the question of the authority given to the Crown in Parliament on matters of worship and doctrine. Mention is made in those paragraphs of the probable filtering of opinion on the way from the parishes to the General Synod. Time will tell whether this fear is justified.

5   The Synodical Government Measure specified proportional representation as the method of election to the General Synod in order to ensure a wide representation of opinion. The fact that in the 1970 elections at least ten dioceses have exercised their right to sub-divide into small electoral areas (single member constituencies in certain dioceses) means that there can be no certainty that the membership of the Synod will faithfully reflect even the broad spectrum of the views of those who do participate actively in Church government. There are also, of course, many other loyal Anglicans who do not so participate, as the electoral roll figures show.

6   I should not necessarily wish to argue as the 1952 Commission did that '. . . the House of Commons represents the mind of the inarticulate mass of laymen more closely than does the House of Laity'. I very much hope that in ten years there will be no grounds for such a view. But while these uncertainties remain there seems some advantage to the Church in leaving residual power in the hands of the Crown in Parliament as a safeguard.

7   A second reason for modification rather than abolition lies in the fact that Parliament is the trustee for our national heritage in which Christianity, and pre-eminently the Church of England, has been a creative factor. It is not inappropriate that the fruitful partnership of Church and State should be expressed by giving to the Crown in Parliament some authority in Church affairs. For Parliament is neither alien nor unsympathetic to the Church. To link the legislatures of Church and State in this way adds to the moral authority of both. Parliament is also able to express the views of the community at large; no other body can represent the mind of the nation so well. Appendix D shows at least that England is not yet anti-Christian and an established Church ought not to ignore the views of the community to which it ministers.

8   Finally, it is not impossible that a demand coming from the Church for the ending of this link might be met in some quarters by a demand for disestablishment, a point made in paragraphs 109 and 110. Indeed, if the

Church argues that the State and its legislature are no longer sufficiently Christian to be allowed even a negative voice in Church affairs, then those who argued for disestablishment on the same grounds would have logic on their side.

One alternative to the present affirmative resolution procedure in Parliament is the negative resolution procedure which is already applied to a wide range of delegated legislation under the provisions of the Statutory Instruments Act 1946 and other Acts. Erskine May's *Parliamentary Practice* describes this (17th edition p. 607) as 'the commonest type of parliamentary control'. By this method Measures would be automatically allowed to take effect upon leaving the General Synod unless they were 'prayed against' in Parliament within a specified time limit. Royal Assent would be signified at a convenient time after the expiration of the 'praying' period.

This procedure was in the original draft of the Enabling Bill but Archbishop Davidson agreed to an amendment in the Lords substituting the affirmative resolution procedure. Since then, pressure of business and the growth of the party system in Parliament has severely limited the power of a private member to 'pray against' matters under the negative resolution procedure. The reality of the situation would be that if a private member wished a Measure from the Synod to be debated he would have to persuade the leaders of one of the main parties to support him. Such a situation could rarely occur. In fact it would only occur in the unlikely event of the Synod passing a Measure against the known wishes of a large section of the Church. Although some members of the Commission have raised practical objections to this alternative, I think it is worth serious consideration and I am assured that it could be viable.

The main objection to the present affirmative resolution procedure is that it brings onto the floors of both Houses of Parliament matters of detail in the management of Church affairs. In other areas of our national life Parliament is no longer required to deal with such details. This compromise ought not to offend those who object to this situation, since under it Parliament could be asked to debate only some very major issue. On the other hand the existence of such a safeguard may go a long way to reassure those who think the Commission's proposals too radical.

I do not regard this alternative as out of line with the overall aims and ideals governing the thinking of the report with which I am in general agreement. On the contrary, I believe that some of these aims are more likely to be attained, and without risk of serious opposition, by the type of modification which I have proposed.

T. E. C. HOARE

The Law of the Church of England

HISTORICAL DEVELOPMENT

1 This Appendix is not limited to ecclesiastical law in the narrow sense of the law administered in ecclesiastical courts, but extends to the wider body of law applicable to and peculiar to the Church of England. This body of law has developed in three historical phases. The first was the pre-Reformation phase, the most relevant part being after the Norman conquest. During this phase the Canon Law of the Western Church including Canons and Constitutions of English synods as well as those coming from Rome and other European sources, was accepted as part of the law of the land. Even during this phase ecclesiastical law was not exclusively Canon Law, but included some customary law and statute law on ecclesiastical matters. When the Reformation came, the Canon Law was preserved by section 7 of the Submission of the Clergy Act 1533 so far as it was not 'contrary or repugnant to the laws, statutes and customs of this realm'. It is not easy to identify the parts of the Canon Law that survived and those that disappeared, but it is clear that the main structure of the Church – its institutions and ecclesiastical offices, the territorial organisation in provinces, dioceses and parishes, the ecclesiastical courts, the holding of property by spiritual corporations, advowsons and the exercise of patronage, were founded in pre-Reformation law that remained part of English law.

2 The Submission of the Clergy Act 1533 severely curtailed the Church's power to legislate by Canon:

   (a) by limiting it to the English Convocations if and when summoned by Royal writ (section 1),

   (b) by requiring the Royal Assent and licence for all Canons (section 1),

   (c) by prohibiting the making of Canons contrary or repugnant to 'the customs, laws or statutes of this realm' (section 3).

   Thirty-two persons appointed under section 2 of the Act should have produced a comprehensive code of surviving Canons which might have been treated as the appropriate field of future legislation by Canon rather than by Statute. In fact no such code was approved, and the eventual limited code of 1603 served little of such purpose. The second phase, therefore, was one of legislation by Statute, ushered in by the group of Acts which separated the English Church from Rome and defined its forms of worship and doctrine. These Acts were followed, over a period of nearly 400 years, by a steady stream of Acts dealing with all aspects of the Church's organisation and property. This body of statute law largely superseded the common law surviving from before the Reformation.

The third and final phase is that of legislation by Church Assembly Measure. The Enabling Act of 1919, which is considered in detail later, enabled the Church Assembly to legislate on all matters concerning the Church of England by Measures which, if approved by both Houses of Parliament, had the force of Acts of Parliament. This Act has been of immense benefit to the Church, which by the close of the last century had become almost immobilised by its legal trammels, and can now move again in the field of law. But the Church of England must still go to Parliament for many matters which other Churches can deal with without going to Parliament. Indeed the field in which such recourse is necessary has become larger as the result of Church Assembly Measures.

THE LAW RELATING TO WORSHIP AND DOCTRINE

The Acts of Uniformity 1548, 1558 and 1662 required the clergy of the Church of England to use the Book of Common Prayer, as first issued in the reign of Edward VI and then revised and expanded and annexed to the Act of 1662, and no other. Section 1 of the last Act also required the morning and evening services contained in that Book to be said in all churches on Sundays. These Acts were reinforced by the Canons of 1603 and the Declaration of Assent in Section 1 of the Clerical Subscription Act 1865, which was required to be taken by all clergymen on ordination and preferment. Now, as the result of the Law Reform (Repeals) Act 1969, and the replacing of the Code of 1603 by the Revised Code of Canons, uniformity of worship rests on the Uniformity Act 1662, the Book of Common Prayer annexed to that Act, the Clerical Subscription Act 1865, and Canons B1 para. 1, and C15, para. 1 of the Revised Code.

An important but temporary change was made in 1965, when the Prayer Book (Alternative and Other Services) Measure 1965 authorised the use, for a period which will effectively end in 1980, of forms of services, alternative to those of the Book of Common Prayer. The forms of services must be approved by Convocations and agreed to by the House of Laity, with a two-thirds majority in all Houses, and must in the opinion of the Convocations be neither contrary to, nor indicative of any departure from, the doctrine of the Church of England. These provisions are contained in section 1 of the Measure, and section 2 authorises trial forms of service. Section 3 provides that the alternative forms of service approved under the Measure are not to be used in any parish without the agreement of the parochial church council. In addition to these main provisions, sections 4 to 7 of the Measure give permanent powers to the Convocations, diocesan bishops and ministers to approve and use services on occasions not provided for in the Book of Common Prayer, and also enable ministers to make minor variations in forms of services, whether in those contained in the Book of Common Prayer or approved under the Measure.

6 The provisions of the Measure have their counterpart in Canons B1 to 5 of the Revised Code of Canons. The provisions were first formulated in draft Canons, and the necessary authorisation by Measure followed. After November 1970, the powers to approve alternative services are exercisable by the General Synod, with a two-thirds majority in all three Houses.

7 As regards doctrine, Canon A5 of the Revised Code of Canons reads as follows:

'The doctrine of the Church of England is grounded in the Holy Scriptures, and in such teachings of the ancient Fathers and Councils of the Church as are agreeable to the said Scriptures. In particular such doctrine is to be found in the Thirty-nine Articles of Religion, the Book of Common Prayer, and the Ordinal.'

Canons 4, 5 and 8 of the Code of 1603 provided for the excommunication of those who impugned the Prayer Book, the Articles or the Ordinal, and section 2 of the Ordination of Ministers Act 1571 provided for the deprivation of clergymen who affirmed any doctrine contrary to the Articles. This latter section was repealed by the Statute Law (Repeals) Act 1969, and the statutory requirement of conformity with the three formularies of the Church of England now rests on the Clerical Subscription Act 1865. This Act not only requires the Declaration of Assent to all three formularies to be made on ordination and preferment, but also provides for the public reading of the Articles by newly-admitted incumbents. These requirements are reproduced in Canon C15 of the Revised Code of Canons.

8 The use by a clergyman of unauthorised forms of worship or a departure from the doctrines of the Church of England constitutes an offence against the laws ecclesiastical for which proceedings may be taken against him in the appropriate ecclesiastical court under the Ecclesiastical Jurisdiction Measure 1963.

CROWN APPOINTMENTS

9 Under the Appointments of Bishops Act 1533 the legal power of choosing archbishops and diocesan bishops lies with the Crown, and under constitutional practice the Sovereign now acts on the advice of the Prime Minister. The Crown issues a licence (*congé d'élire*) to the

appropriate dean and chapter to elect the person nominated by the Crown, which they are required to do within 12 days; the election is then certified to the Crown and, in the case of a vacant bishopric, is notified by the Crown to the Archbishop, who is required to confirm the election and consecrate the person elected; in the case of a vacant archbishopric, the notification is to the other Archbishop and two bishops or to four bishops, and the confirmation and consecration is by them. If the dean and chapter fail to elect the person nominated within 12 days, the Crown may by Letters Patent nominate and present to the Archbishop or, in the case of a vacant archbishopric, to the other Archbishop and two bishops or the four bishops, who are required to carry out the consecration. Until recently persons who refused to carry out an election or consecration under the Act were liable to the pains and penalties of *Praemunire*, but this obsolete sanction was abolished by the Criminal Law Act 1967.

Suffragan bishops are appointed under the Suffragan Bishops Act 1534. The diocesan bishop submits two names to the Sovereign, one of whom is presented by Letters Patent for consecration by the Archbishop. In practice the first name submitted is always chosen.

Deans of cathedrals are appointed by the Crown by Letters Patent. Before the Ecclesiastical Commissioners Act 1840 those of the old foundation were appointed under the *congé d'élire* procedure, but section 24 of that Act provided for their appointment by Letters Patent, which is the customary method in the case of deans of the new foundation. Similar provision is made in the case of deans of new cathedrals created by recent statutes.

Some canonries and a considerable number of livings are in the patronage of the Crown, which is exercised in the same way as private patronage. In the case of livings not exceeding an annual value of £20 in the King's Book (a compilation of Henry VIII), the presentation is made by the Lord Chancellor. The Crown also exercises patronage in the case of other livings, when the rights of a private patron and the bishop have lapsed, or there is incapacity of the patron.

ECCLESIASTICAL COURTS

The Reformation Acts, in particular the Act of Supremacy, abolished the ecclesiastical jurisdiction of the Pope in respect of matters arising in this country and vested all spiritual and ecclesiastical jurisdiction in the King. The ecclesiastical courts, i.e. the consistory and provincial courts, were thus established as courts of the Crown, just as much as the secular courts. Appeals from the provincial courts lay to the King in Chancery and were heard by a specially constituted court known as the Court of Delegates. This appellate jurisdiction was transferred in 1833 to the Judicial Committee of the Privy Council.

14 Ecclesiastical courts formerly possessed considerable secular jurisdiction in matrimonial and testamentary matters and defamation but this jurisdiction was transferred to the secular courts in the middle of the nineteenth century. They also had powers to try lay persons for ecclesiastical and moral offences. The latter jurisdiction was judicially declared in 1876 to be inconsistent with modern custom and opinion, but was thought to survive as respects lay officers of the Church. It was, however, finally abolished by section 82 of the Ecclesiastical Jurisdiction Measure 1963.

15 This comprehensive Measure sets out the constitution of the present ecclesiastical courts and their jurisdiction. The latter is now for practical purposes limited to:

(a) disciplinary proceedings against bishops and clergy, which may either be cases of unbecoming conduct or neglect of duty, or cases involving matters of doctrine, ritual or ceremonial;

(b) faculty proceedings, which also may involve matters of doctrine, ritual or ceremonial.

To try these proceedings the Measure provides a structure of courts:

(i) Disciplinary 'conduct' proceedings against archbishops and bishops are tried by commissions appointed by Convocations and consisting of four diocesan bishops presided over by the Dean of Arches and Auditor with an appeal to a Commission of Review appointed by the Crown and consisting of three Lords of Appeal who are communicants and two bishops who are members of the House of Lords.

(ii) Disciplinary 'conduct' proceedings against the clergy are tried by consistory courts, with an appeal to provincial courts and no further appeal.

(iii) All disciplinary proceedings involving matters of doctrine, ritual and ceremonial are tried by the new Court of Ecclesiastical Causes Reserved appointed by the Crown and consisting of two persons who have held high judicial office and are communicants and three diocesan bishops, with an appeal to a Commission of Review, who in doctrine cases are assisted by five advisers drawn from a panel of diocesan bishops and theologians.

(iv) Faculty proceedings involving matters of doctrine, ritual or ceremonial are tried by consistory courts, with an appeal to the Court of Ecclesiastical Causes Reserved and a further appeal to a Commission of Review, as above.

(v) Faculty proceedings not involving such matters are tried by consistory courts, with an appeal to provincial courts and a further appeal to the Privy Council. This is the only appellate jurisdiction now exercised by the Privy Council.

Since the Measure passed, one 'conduct' case against an incumbent has gone to trial and appeal, and in other such cases the accused has submitted to judgement by the bishop under section 31. No proceedings involving matters of doctrine etc. have been instituted.

THE SOVEREIGN AS SUPREME GOVERNOR

The position and powers of the Crown in respect of the making of Canons, the appointment of bishops and other dignitaries, and ecclesiastical jurisdiction has already been referred to. There remain certain more formal matters concerning the position of the Sovereign in relation to the Church. The title of 'supreme Head of the Church of England' was given to the King by the Act of 26 Henry 8 cap. 1 which was repealed in the reign of Mary and not revived by the Act of Supremacy. The latter Act refrained from using this title, and laid emphasis on the Sovereign's supremacy in the sphere of ecclesiastical jurisdiction. The oath of supremacy required by section 9 of the Act to be taken by the clergy described the Sovereign as the supreme governor of the realm in all spiritual and ecclesiastical causes as well as temporal. The declaration of King Charles I prefixed to the Thirty-nine Articles in the Book of Common Prayer described him as the Supreme Governor of the Church of England.

The present oath of allegiance, taken by a clergyman under the Clerical Subscription Act 1865 on ordination or preferment and by an archbishop or bishop before consecration or translation, simply requires him to be faithful and bear true allegiance to Her Majesty, and is in the same terms as the oath taken by Members of Parliament and the holders of various public and judicial offices under the Promissory Oaths Act 1868.

Article 37 of the Thirty-nine Articles makes it clear that the Sovereign's position does not give him the spiritual status of a Minister of the Word.

Section 2 of the Act of Settlement requires the Sovereign to take a coronation oath in the form provided by the Coronation Oath Act 1688 and modified by subsequent enactments. The present oath requires the Sovereign to promise, among other things, to maintain the laws of God, the true provision of the Gospel, and the Protestant reformed religion established by law; to maintain and preserve inviolably the settlement of the Church of England and the doctrine, worship, discipline and government thereof, as by law established in England; and to preserve unto the bishops and clergy of England and to the Church therein committed to their charge, all such rights and privileges as by law do or shall appertain unto them or any of them. In addition the Act of Settlement and the Bill of Rights require the Sovereign to join in communion with the Church of England, and to make on accession a declaration, now in the form scheduled to the

Accession Declaration Act 1910, that he is a faithful Protestant and will uphold the enactments securing the Protestant accession to the Throne.

20 The Sovereign is said to be the supreme ordinary and visitor, and as such visits archbishops and receives their resignations. The Sovereign is the ordinary and visitor of royal peculiars, i.e. Westminster Abbey, Saint George's Chapel, Windsor, and the Chapels Royal.

MEMBERSHIP OF PARLIAMENT

21 The archbishops and 24 bishops of the Church of England have seats in the House of Lords by ancient usage; they were temporarily excluded in the seventeenth century, and their numbers were temporarily altered between the union with Ireland and the disestablishment of the Irish Church. The archbishops, the bishops of London, Durham and Winchester always have seats, and the other bishops are chosen by seniority of appointment to a diocesan see.

22 Church of England clergymen are disqualified from sitting in the House of Commons by the House of Commons (Clergy Disqualification) Act 1801. According to some opinion there was previously a common law disqualification, the ground for it being that till 1667 the clergy were taxed by Convocation and not by the Commons. Justification for the statutory disqualification was based in 1801 upon the great number of clergy whose livings were in the gift of the Crown or the nobility, which might affect the independence of the House of Commons.

THE ENABLING ACT

23 The Church of England Assembly (Powers) Act 1919 (commonly referred to as the 'Enabling Act') did not constitute the Church Assembly. Its constitution was prepared by a representative body set up by the Convocations and was then appended to the Addresses of the Convocations recited in the preamble to the Act. Nor did the Act in terms confer power on the Assembly to pass Measures; this was comprised in the general power under Article 14 of the Constitution to discuss and make provision for matters concerning the Church of England and, if parliamentary sanction were required, to seek it in 'such manner as may be prescribed by statute'. The Enabling Act was therefore concerned with the procedure for giving parliamentary approval and statutory force to Measures passed by the Assembly under its own constitution.

24 The procedure is set out in sections 3 and 4 of the Act. Measures are submitted, with comments and explanations, by the Legislative Committee of the Assembly to a joint Committee of both Houses of Parliament called the Ecclesiastical Committee. The latter Committee

considers the Measure and may hold a conference with the Legislative Committee. The Ecclesiastical Committee reports to Parliament on the Measure, but, before doing so, communicates the draft report to the Legislative Committee. The latter has no power to amend the Measure to meet any criticism made in the report, but may withdraw the Measure. Otherwise it is laid before both Houses, with the report of the Ecclesiastical Committee, and on a resolution being passed by each House, is presented to Her Majesty. The Royal Assent is then signified in the same manner as to Acts of Parliament, and the Measure has the same force and effect as an Act. By virtue of an express provision in section 3 (6) of the Enabling Act a Measure may amend or repeal any Act of Parliament, including the Enabling Act itself, but cannot alter the composition or powers and duties of the Ecclesiastical Committee or the procedure in Parliament prescribed in section 4 of the Act.

5 The absence of a power of amendment by the Legislative Committee has been embarrassing on a few occasions, but it would be difficult to give such a power in respect of Measures passed by the Assembly in accordance with a three-stage procedure usually spread over more than a year. On one recent occasion the difficulty was met by using the power of the Chairman of Committees and the Chairman of Ways and Means to divide a Measure under the proviso to section 4 of the Enabling Act. The power to withdraw a Measure may, now that the General Synod has succeeded the Church Assembly, become of greater use than hitherto, by virtue of a proposed new procedure for carrying out a limited amendment by the Synod of a Measure so withdrawn and re-submitting it to the Ecclesiastical Committee.

6 Section 3 (3) of the Enabling Act requires the Ecclesiastical Committee to state its views on the expediency of a Measure 'especially with relation to the constitutional rights of all His Majesty's subjects'. This phrase has been much discussed, and it is thought to mean the rights of the people of England, and not merely those who take an active part in church affairs or are regular church-goers, to worship when they wish in their parish churches and to receive the sacraments and ministrations of the parish clergy. These rights have been upheld in cases in the courts, and they are also guaranteed by the parochial system extending over the whole country and by the obligations involved in the cure of souls.

THE REVISED CODE OF CANONS

7 The revision of the Canons began with the Archbishops' Commission on Canon Law who reported in 1947. Their task was to sift the operative Canons (pre-Reformation and post-Reformation) from those which could be regarded as obsolete, and to prepare a revised body of operative Canons. The Commission found that the sifting process would involve much research into pre-Reformation Canon Law, and that the

expense would not be justified. They decided, therefore, to prepare a limited code, based on the 1603 code, which would not claim to be exhaustive but would cover 'those aspects of Church life which are most suitably treated by law in canonical form'. An indication of the scope of the code that was finally completed and issued in 1969 is given by a list of the sections:

(a) The Church of England (covering its apostolic authority, formularies and the royal supremacy).

(b) Divine Service and the Administration of the Sacraments.

(c) Ministers, their Ordination, Function and Charge.

(d) The Order of Deaconesses.

(e) The Lay Officers of the Church of England.

(f) Things Appertaining to Churches.

(g) The Ecclesiastical Courts.

(h) Synodical Government.

28 The revised Canons cover some matters which are also the subject of statutory provision (or rubrics having statutory force). The purpose of covering these matters is to make the code reasonably complete in its chosen fields, and to give canonical authority in those fields. Sometimes the Canons duplicate, almost verbatim, the statutory provisions, and at other times (notably in the section on the Ecclesiastical Courts) they endorse the statutory provisions by reference.

29 Under section 3 of the Submission of the Clergy Act 1533, Canons must not be contrary or repugnant to the royal prerogative or the customs, laws or statutes of this realm. Accordingly, when the proposed new Canons involved changes in matters governed by statutes or rubrics, it was necessary to effect the changes by Measure before they could be incorporated in the Canons. Three Prayer Book Measures and three other Measures were passed for this purpose during the years 1964 to 1968. One Measure, the Holy Table Measure 1964, was passed in order to override decisions of ecclesiastical courts in faculty proceedings. These Measures only covered specific matters. If further changes are proposed to be made by future Canons which impinge on statute law or case law, further authorisation by Measure will be needed before the Canons can be made. This dual process, as hitherto operated *ad hoc* and piecemeal, has proved laborious. If legislation by Canon is to be effective and the new code kept up-to-date, as the Church seems to desire, it is necessary to give more general authorisations, in the appropriate fields, to make changes in the law by Canon, and to repeal statutes encroaching on those fields.

30 Section 1 of the Submission of the Clergy Act 1533 (see paragraph 2 above) has not impeded canon law revision. Convocations can no longer (even in theory) be suspended, because by section 1 (3) of the

Church of England Convocations Act 1966 Her Majesty is required to summon new Convocations as soon as may be convenient after the dissolution of the old. The intention of the Act is that a dissolution and election will take place at regular 5-year intervals, and this will apply to the General Synod as well as the Convocations. As regards the requirement of the Royal Assent and licence, it is clear that the Crown's advisers have only concerned themselves with the question whether the Canons comply with section 3 of the Act, i.e. are consistent with the Royal prerogative and the common law and statutes. On this question they have not disagreed on any point with the views expressed by the advisers of the Church.

There is one other point that should be mentioned. The Canons of 1603 were held not to bind the laity *proprio vigore* – by their own force and authority, but only to bind the clergy in *re ecclesiastica*. The leading case is *Middleton v Crofts* (1736 2 Atkins 650) approved by the House of Lords in the *Bishop of Exeter v Marshall* (2 L.R. 3 H.L. 17). The circumstances of Middleton and Crofts could not apply today. Ecclesiastical courts then had jurisdiction over the laity in matrimonial matters and the Middletons were articled in the Hereford Consistory Court for, among other matters, getting married outside the canonical hours of 8 a.m. to 12 noon, a limitation not found in the civil law. It was held that this canonical rule did not bind the parties to the marriage, and the proceedings in the Consistory court were prohibited, so far as that matter was concerned.

This rule, if it had applied, would have made the parties liable to penalties in the ecclesiastical courts for a breach of the rule. Nowadays the ecclesiastical courts have no penal jurisdiction over the laity and no means of enforcing obligations against them, except those arising out of faculty proceedings, and so Canons cannot have any coercive effect against the laity. The question, however, arises whether Middleton *v* Crofts allows Canons to lay down rules for the Church which apply to the laity in much the same way as the rules of a voluntary society. The revised Canons assume that this is so. Thus Canon B 20 of the revised Canons gives to the minister the final responsibility for ordering the music of the Church. This means that parties to a marriage cannot have an absolute right to choose the music; they must accept this as a condition of getting married in a church of the Church of England. Sections D and E of the revised Canons lay down the rules governing the admission and licensing of deaconesses and lay readers and the ministry and offices that they can perform. Lay people who voluntarily seek these offices do so on the basis of these rules, which they accept. If they break the rules, their licences can be terminated, but they are not subject to penalties. These Canons were in fact based on previous resolutions of the Convocations, which would have been equally effective for practical purposes if accepted as authoritative rulings of the

Church. The Canons could only give some additional authority, and a rather theoretical penal sanction on the clergy if they allowed deaconesses or lay readers to exceed their functions. Therefore the decision in Middleton *v* Crofts does not stand in the way of the future use of Canons as the appropriate instrument for laying down the rules of the Church in the sphere of worship and ministry.

THE SYNODICAL GOVERNMENT MEASURE 1969

33 This Measure unites in the General Synod the functions of the Church Assembly and the Convocations, so that the House of Laity will in future play a full part in matters hitherto the sole or primary responsibility of the Convocations, such as the making of Canons and liturgical revision. Although the House of Laity of the Assembly were fully consulted during Canon Law revision, and their agreement is required for new forms of service, the process of consultation or reaching agreement between separate bodies is much more difficult and less satisfactory than the process of common deliberation and decision.

34 The Measure considerably reduces the size of the General Synod, as compared with the Church Assembly, and also provides for setting up diocesan and deanery synods which are expected to be more effective bodies and provide better channels of communication than the present diocesan conferences and deanery conferences. All the synods have now been constituted.

35 Article 6 of the Constitution of the General Synod in Schedule 2 to the Measure sets out the powers to legislate by Measure and Canon, and also refers to powers of subordinate legislation authorised by Measure or Canon, and powers to issue other instruments of moral authority but not having the force of law. This is little more than an express recognition of existing practice, but may lead to the avoidance of detailed legislation by Measure or Canon on matters which can properly be dealt with by subordinate or non-legislative instruments. This matter is considered further in chapter 5 of this Report, which reviews a wide field of church law relating to pastoral organisation, the patronage system and church property.

Draft of a Measure

To enable provision to be made by Canon with respect to the forms of worship used in the Church of England and other matters prescribed by the Book of Common Prayer, and with respect to the obligations and forms of subscription to the doctrine of the Church of England and the interpretation of that doctrine; to repeal the enactments relating to the matters aforesaid; and for purposes connected therewith.

1. (1) It shall be lawful for the General Synod to make provision by Canon with respect to the forms of worship to be used in the Church of England, *including provision for amending or superseding the forms of worship contained in the Book of Common Prayer or any of them.*

Provision by Canon for worship in the Church of England.

(Alternative to words in italics[1])

but such provision shall preserve the availability of the forms of worship contained in the Book of Common Prayer for use in any parish where it is decided to use them or any of them.

(2) It shall also be lawful for the General Synod to provide by Canon for revoking or amending any of the rubrics contained in the Book of Common Prayer (but not comprised in forms of worship) and for any matters to which such rubrics relate.

(3) No Canon making any such provision as aforesaid shall be submitted for Her Majesty's Licence and Assent unless it has been approved by the General Synod with a majority in each House thereof of not less than two-thirds of those present and voting; and all powers conferred by any such Canon to approve, amend, continue or discontinue any form of worship shall be exercisable by the General Synod with such a majority as aforesaid in each House thereof and not otherwise.

(4) Where alternative forms of worship are authorised or approved by or under Canon, it shall be provided by Canon that decisions as to which forms of worship are to be used in any parish shall be taken jointly by the incumbent and the parochial church council, and, in case of disagreement, by the bishop of the diocese.

(5) No provision made by or under Canon with respect to the Book of Common Prayer shall affect the authority of that Book

---

[1]The alternatives correspond with the two points of view set out in paragraph 73 of the Report.

in its original form as a historic formulary of doctrine interpreted in accordance with the next following section.[1]

Subscription to and interpretation of doctrine.

2. (1) It shall be lawful for the General Synod to make provision by Canon:

(*a*) with respect to the obligations of the clergy, deaconesses and lay officers of the Church of England to subscribe to the doctrine of that Church, and the forms of that subscription; and

(*b*) for interpreting, whether by the forms of subscription or otherwise, the formularies of the Church of England, that is to say the Thirty-nine Articles of Religion and the Book of Common Prayer, and in particular for interpreting them in their historical context and in relation to other understandings of Christian truth.

(2) In this section 'lay officers' means readers, lay judges of consistory and provincial courts, and lay holders of other offices admission to which is for the time being regulated by Canon.

Safeguarding of doctrine.

3. (1) Every form of worship or amendment thereof authorised or approved by or under any Canon and every other provision made by or under any Canon in respect of the matters mentioned in the preceding provisions of this Measure shall be such as in the opinion of the General Synod is neither contrary to, nor indicative of any departure from, the doctrine of the Church of England in any essential matter.

(2) The final approval by the General Synod of any such form of worship or amendment thereof or other such provision as aforesaid shall conclusively determine that the Synod is of such opinion as aforesaid with respect to the matter so approved.

Repeal of enactments and amendment of Submission of Clergy Act 1533.

4. (1) The Acts and Measures specified in the Schedule to this Measure are hereby repealed to the extent specified in column 3 thereof.

(2) As respects any matters to which the provisions so repealed relate, other than matters for which provision is made by the preceding sections of this Measure, the effect of the repeal shall be to leave those matters to be provided for by Canon, and to enable any existing Canons relating to those matters to be amended or revoked by Canon, without the need of any statutory provision.

(3) Section 3 of the Submission of the Clergy Act 1533 (which provides that no Canons shall be contrary to the royal prerogative

---

[1]This sub-section is only needed if the first alternative is adopted, because the importance of the Book of Common Prayer as a formulary of doctrine lies in the services themselves, which would be preserved under the second alternative.

he customs, laws or statutes of this realm) shall not apply to any
: of ecclesiastical law relating to any matter for which provision
y be made by Canon in pursuance of this Measure.

Inter-
pretation.

In this Measure the following expressions have the meanings
eby assigned to them:

ok of Common Prayer' means the Book annexed to the Act
f Uniformity 1662 and entitled 'The Book of Common Prayer
nd Administration of the Sacraments and other Rites and
Ceremonies of the Church according to the use of the Church of
England together with the Psalter or Psalms of David appointed
s they are to be sung or said in Churches and the Form and
Manner of Making, Ordaining and Consecrating Bishops,
riests and Deacons';

m of worship' means any order, service, prayer, rite or cere-
nony whatsoever, including the Form and Manner of Making,
laining and Consecrating Bishops, Priests and Deacons;

rics' of the Book of Common Prayer include all directions and
nstructions contained in the said Book, whether or not com-
rised in forms of worship, and all prefaces, tables, rules, calen-
ars and other contents of the said Book not comprised in
orms of worship.

This Measure shall come into force on such day as the Arch-
ops of Canterbury and York may jointly appoint:
Provided that the powers to make Canons in pursuance of this
asure shall be exercisable before the appointed day, but no
n Canon shall come into operation before the appointed day.

Commence-
ment of
Measure.

This Measure may be cited as the Church of England (Worship
Doctrine) Measure 19—.

Short Title.

SCHEDULE

Acts and Measures Repealed

SESSION AND CHAPTER	SHORT TITLE	EXTENT OF REPEAL
2 & 3 Edw. 6 c.1.	The Act of Uniformity 1548.	The whole Act, so far as unrepealed.
1 Eliz. 1 c.2.	The Act of Uniformity 1558	The whole Act, so far as repealed.
13 Eliz. 1 c.12.	The Ordination of Ministers Act 1571.	The whole Act.
14 Cha. 2 c.4.	The Act of Uniformity 1662.	The whole Act.
28 & 29 Vict. c.122.	The Clerical Subscription Act 1865.	Section 1, and other sections so far as they relate to the Declaration of Assent and and the Thirty-nine Articles.
34 & 35 Vict. c.26.	The Universities Tests Act 1871.	Section 6, so far as it restricts to week-days only the use of adaptations or abridgements of the Book of Common Prayer.
35 & 36 Vict. c.35.	The Act of Uniformity Amendment Act 1872.	The whole Act.
15 & 16 Geo. 6 & 1 Eliz. 2 c.xxxviii	The City of London (Guild Churches) Act 1952.	Section 8 (4) & (5).
11 & 12 Eliz. 2 No. 1	The Ecclesiastical Jurisdiction Measure 1963.	Sections 2 (5), 3 (6) and (7), and 27 (2), so far as they relate to the declaration scheduled to the Measure, and Part II of Schedule 1.

SESSION AND CHAPTER	SHORT TITLE	EXTENT OF REPEAL
12 & 13 Eliz. 2 No. 4	The Holy Table Measure 1964.	The whole Measure.
12 & 13 Eliz. 2 No. 6	The Clergy (Ordination and Miscellaneous Provisions) Measure 1964.	Part I and in section 12 the words 'in subsection (2) of section four'.
12 & 13 Eliz. 2 No. 7	The Vestures of Ministers Measure 1964.	The whole Measure.
13 & 14 Eliz. 2 No. 1	The Prayer Book (Alternative and Other Services) Measure 1965.	The whole Measure.
13 & 14 Eliz. 2 No. 3	The Prayer Book (Miscellaneous Provisions) Measure 1965.	The whole Measure.
16 & 17 Eliz. 2 No. 1	The Pastoral Measure 1968.	Section 74 and section 75 (2).
16 & 17 Eliz. 2 No. 2	The Prayer Book (Further Provisions) Measure 1968.	The whole Measure.

Suggestions Supplementary to Chapter 3

APPOINTMENT OF BISHOPS

1 If there were a Church Advisory Committee, or an Electoral Board, the General Synod should appoint a standing panel from which its representatives on the Committee or Board should be chosen, according to strict rules. When duly constituted, the Committee or Board would have the services of the Archbishops' Appointments Secretary as an adviser. Anyone would be free to suggest a name for consideration by the Committee or Board. The members, and their officers, would be bound by a strict requirement of confidentiality. The Appointments Secretary, while he would be present at its meetings, would not be formally a member or free to take part in its deliberations beyond his activities as adviser. Some other person, possibly the Legal Secretary of the Archbishop of the Province, should act as Secretary to the Committee or Board.

2 Those who wish to end the responsibility of the Prime Minister envisage that the Electoral Board having made its choice would submit only one name which could be transmitted by the Archbishop to the Sovereign. Whether the Sovereign would approve in the present manner, that is by issuing Letters Patent and a licence to consecrate, would be for consideration. If an electoral board thus elected the bishop, the diocese would have been represented, both in the advice given beforehand through the Vacancy-in-See Committee, and on the electoral board itself. If the responsibility of the Prime Minister ended in that way there would be no need for a diocesan election by the dean and chapter or other electoral body, and such forms of election would cease.

ARCHBISHOPS

3 In the choice of an archbishop there would need to be modifications in detail designed to give greater representation to a wider constituency.

4 In the case of a vacancy in the See of Canterbury the chairman of the Committee or Board might be a lay communicant Anglican appointed by the Prime Minister and the members should include the Archbishop of York or his nominee, the Executive Officer of the Anglican Communion, two diocesan bishops, together with two clergymen and two laymen appointed by the General Synod and four members appointed

by the Vacancy-in-See Committee of the Diocese. In the case of York the Archbishop of Canterbury would replace the Archbishop of York or his nominee and the Anglican Executive Officer need not be a member.

OTHER CROWN APPOINTMENTS

There remains the question of Crown patronage of deaneries and canonries and livings. We agree with the Howick Commission in regarding this as, in essence, no different from any other form of patronage, and that a solution should be sought in the context of the general adaptation of the patronage system. But we have not sought to make recommendations about deaneries, canonries and livings. The General Synod will need to consider these matters further in accordance with its mode of advance on the questions of diocesan bishops on the one side and the general system of pastoral care on the other.

Consideration might be given at the same time to the appointment by the Crown of two of the three Church Estates Commissioners.

APPENDIX D

Church and Society

The Commission was able, through the generosity of the Joseph Rowntree Memorial Trust and the Church of England Central Board of Finance, to mount a study of existing material, both published and unpublished, on religious belief and practice in England. This project served a double function: it provided a necessary information service for the Commission, and it laid a foundation for future research by collating scattered material in a new and relatively undeveloped area in the social sciences. The summarised report which is given below has been prepared by Professor Kathleen Jones (a member of the Commission), Mr. R. W. Coles and Dr C. B. Campbell, all of the University of York, who worked together on the project. Their views do not necessarily represent those of the Commission as a whole.

1 There has been only one general census of church attendance in England: the census carried out, under the supervision of Horace Mann, on the last Sunday in March, 1851. 10.4 million attendances were reported during the day, half of them in Anglican churches. Assuming that this was a typical Sunday for attendance purposes (it was the fourth Sunday in Lent) this suggests that 40 per cent of the adult population went to church, and 20 per cent (half the total) to Anglican churches.[1] These figures relate to a period generally considered to be one of religious revival. They can be set against a modern estimate, made by Dr David Martin, which suggests that about 25 per cent of the population now goes to church once a month or more, half these going to Anglican churches.[2] If the heyday of Victorian churchgoing was less golden than it is sometimes said to be – for it appears that even in 1851, attendance at church was a minority activity – the decline to the present level of attendance is correspondingly less sharp.

2 However, even simple statements of this order require very careful qualification. If our modern techniques of enquiry are more sophisticated than Horace Mann's, they still have many limitations, and require very cautious interpretation of the results.

3 There are now three main sources of evidence: opinion surveys, official church statistics, and local surveys. Since each offers evidence of a different kind, it is necessary to consider them separately.

---

[1] H. Mann, Census of 1851 (c. 1690) : Report on Religious Worship.
[2] D. Martin: *A Sociology of English Religion*. SCM Press, 1967, p. 43. This would include attendance at the occasional offices and on such special days as Harvest Festival or Remembrance Sunday.

Opinion polls represent what people say they do and believe when confronted by a professional interviewer with a questionnaire. They rely on sampling techniques, and the results claimed are therefore only approximate when applied to the whole population. The categories used for age, social class and so on are often very broad, and the findings consequently very generalised. Replies are often classified in terms of 'Yes/No/Don't know', and even the more sophisticated surveys cannot usually allow for the expression of fine shades of meaning.

The techniques of opinion polls work well enough for market research, which is their main application. They work less well for complex questions such as those involved in religious belief and practice. As a general rule, the more factual the question, the more reliable the answer – e.g. 'Did you go to church last Sunday?' is likely to produce better material than 'Do you believe in a personal God or a life-force?'.

The limitations of opinion polls in the social analysis of religion have been discussed by Dr Bernice Martin in *Comments on Some Gallup Poll Statistics*.[1] She concludes that, despite the limited and subjective nature of the material, the results yielded on broad issues are remarkably congruent.

CHURCH AFFILIATION

An analysis of data from nine Gallup Poll surveys carried out between 1963 and 1967 showed fairly consistent figures for Church affiliation: 'The C. of E. varies between almost 57 per cent and almost 64 per cent; Nonconformity between almost 9 per cent and over 12 per cent; Roman Catholicism between 10 per cent and almost 13 per cent.'[2]

These surveys included Scotland, and the percentage of members of the Church of England is therefore lower than it would be in a survey confined to the two provinces of Canterbury and York.

The most detailed survey material on religious belief and practice to become available in recent years is that produced for the television authorities – the ABC Television survey undertaken by Social Surveys (Gallup Poll) Ltd, in 1964 and the survey undertaken for the Independent Television Authority by the Opinion Research Centre in 1968.[3] The 1964 survey was based on two samples (*a*) a stratified sample of persons aged 16 and over living in the London, Midlands and Northern

---

[1] In D. Martin (ed): *Sociological Yearbook of Religion in England*. SCM Press, 1968.
[2] D. Martin (ed), *Op. Cit.*, p. 150.
[3] The 1964 Survey is reported in *Television and Religion*, University of London Press, 1964 and statistical tables are available from ABC Television Ltd. These are quoted by permission of ABC Television. The 1968 survey is available in statistical form from the Opinion Research Centre, Albany Buildings, 47 Victoria Street, London SW1, and is quoted by permission of the Independent Television Authority. (Now published as *Religion in Britain and Northern Ireland*, ITA, 1970.)

Independent television areas, and (b) a random sample of the population of England and Wales. These gave the following percentages in answer to the question 'To what religious denomination do you belong?'

Religious classification	1964 Survey (a) %	1964 Survey (b) %
Church of England	67	68
Nonconformist	13	12
Roman Catholic	9	10
Other	5	5
None	6	5

10 The projected total population of England (i.e. the provinces of Canterbury and York) for 1968 was 45,863,000.[1] A round figure of 46 million has been taken for the very generalised estimates which appear in the text of the Commission's Report, and which are explained as follows: applying the average of the figures given above to a population of 46 million, we obtain the following estimates:

Religious classification	% average of (a) and (b) above	Estimated no. (million) in pop. of 46 million
Church of England	67·5	31·0
Nonconformist	12·5	5·7
Roman Catholic	9·5	4·3
Other	5·0	2·3
None	5·5	2·7

11 The 1964 survey also included material on the age, sex and social class of those claiming Anglican, Free Church or Roman Catholic affiliation, and comments:

'It is apparent that the strength of the Church of England is derived from the fact that it represents all groups of society. Irrespective of the characteristic that is being used for analysis, the Church of England can claim that between 64 per cent and 70 per cent of the population will belong to it . . . in every way it represents a complete cross-section of the population'.[2]

12 The following percentages of the survey population in each age group claimed to be members of the Church of England:

67 per cent of the 16–24 year olds.
68 per cent of the 25–34 year olds.
66 per cent of the 35–44 year olds.
67 per cent of those aged 45 and over.

---

[1]Table A4, Registrar-General's Statistical Review of England and Wales, 1968, Part II.
[2]*Television and Religion*, 1964, pp. 11–12.

Full figures for other denominations are not given either in the text of the book or in the separately-published statistical tables, but it is stated that the Nonconformists are strongest in the oldest age group, and the Roman Catholics in the youngest.[1]

Sex: Church of England affiliation was claimed by 65 per cent of all men and 69 per cent of all women. Nonconformist affiliation was claimed by 14 per cent and 13 per cent respectively, and Roman Catholic affiliation by 9 per cent of each sex.

Social class: The definitions of social class are the very broad ones used by Gallup Poll Ltd, and not the more detailed ones based on the Registrar-General's Social Class Index. The Church of England was represented by 67 per cent of the upper socio-economic class group and 67 per cent of the lower class group; the Nonconformists by 13 per cent of the upper and 14 per cent of the lower group; the Roman Catholics by 8 per cent of the upper and 10 per cent of the lower group.

In the 1968 survey, the proportion of Anglican adherents was strikingly lower:

Are you a member of a Church, faith or religion?	1968 *survey* %
No	22
If yes, which one?	
Church of England	50
Nonconformist	14
Roman Catholic	9
Other	5

On this basis, the estimated number of nominal Anglicans in the population would not be above 23 million, and we have used this figure as the minimum estimate in the text of the Report. However, the sample for this survey was drawn from the whole of Great Britain, and could therefore be expected to contain a lower percentage of Anglicans than those for the 1964 survey, which were confined to the ITV regions and England and Wales. In addition, the question about church affiliation was asked in a different form. In 1964, the question was 'What religious denomination do you belong to?' which has a slight bias towards a positive answer. In 1968, the question was 'Are you a member of a church, faith, or religion?' and this clearly attracted a larger proportion of negative answers.

The exact size and strength of the Church of England's nominal adherence is therefore in some doubt, but it is safe to say that it comprises at least half and probably two-thirds of the population of England.

---

[1]This is supported in R. Goldman, *New Society*, May 27th, 1965.

19 The 1964 television survey produced a variety of statistics on church attendance, but these are difficult to interpret. Weekly church attendance at all places of worship was reported at 10 per cent of the population.

20 If 10 per cent now go to church on a typical Sunday, how are they composed as between denominations? We are told that 7 per cent of Church of England members went to church on the Sunday in question as against 20 per cent of Nonconformists and 23 per cent of Roman Catholics. Out of our 46 million, between 23 and 30 million call themselves 'C. of E.' and this suggests that between one and a half and rather more than two million people attend Anglican churches on an average Sunday. Corresponding figures for Nonconformists and Roman Catholics would be approximately just over one million and just under one million. As the report notes, the rate of weekly church going as against claimed membership is particularly low in the Church of England; but the numbers claiming membership are so large that even a low rate still results in considerable figures for attendance.

21 There is another aspect which is worth attention: according to the 1964 survey, of those claiming to be Church of England, 7 per cent went to church on the previous Sunday, but 13 per cent claimed to attend on two or more Sundays a month. Some observers consider that monthly attendance is now a better index of churchgoing than weekly attendance, at least for Anglicans, and that the numbers attending on any one Sunday may be a half or less of those who regard themselves as regular churchgoers. If this is so, then the numbers 'regularly' attending Anglican churches are considerably in excess of the numbers of Easter communicants (a point to which we return in considering Communion statistics). Dr David Martin's conclusion that 25 per cent of the population goes to church about once a month, and that about half (i.e. $12\frac{1}{2}$ per cent) go to an Anglican church is generally supported by this, as by other opinion surveys, though much work remains to be done before such estimates can be more than the most crude of approximations.

22 Other findings of the 1968 television survey make interesting reading. Eighty per cent of the sample thought that God created the universe; 85 per cent thought that Jesus was the Son of God; 81 per cent thought it was important that Britain should be a Christian country; 37 per cent agreed with the statement 'I am not a religious person'; 80 per cent admired clergymen 'quite a lot' or 'a great deal' but only 30 per cent looked forward to meeting them. There are hints here both of the confusions caused by the crudity of the method, and of the very real ambivalence which religion seems to call forth; but the figures, despite their limitations, give no ground for the contention that religion is now a minority interest in a secular society.

Official statistics of membership are issued by most religious organisations in annual yearbooks. In the *Church of England Yearbook*, figures are based on parochial and diocesan returns. They include information on church membership in terms of baptisms, confirmations, marriages, Easter and Christmas communicants and electoral roll registration. Facts and Figures about the Church of England, published by the Church Statistical Office, gives more detailed material, including analyses of information by dioceses and over periods of years.

This material is highly reliable, being based on total returns, and, in the case of baptisms and marriages, on individual returns. It is very competently processed by the Church Information Office. However, as sociological data, it is of limited use for three reasons:

1. Because the mode of data collection is through parish and diocesan organisation, it is for ecclesiastical areas, and the data can neither be compared with census data (based on enumeration districts with different boundaries) nor with data from the other Churches, which collect information on the basis of their own areas of jurisdiction.

2. While the material is exact, it is not always comprehensive. It is based on parochial returns, and excludes extra-parochial establishments such as Royal Peculiars, Chapels Royal, chapels in hospitals, schools, colleges and Forces establishments, retreat houses and religious communities. This can lead to an underestimation of baptisms and Easter Day communicants.

3. Each religious body has its own criteria for membership, and these differ considerably from each other in emphasis. Also some observers have expressed a doubt as to whether purely denominational modes of information collection are appropriate in an increasingly ecumenical age. Some people, particularly those in the younger generation, feel a reluctance to wear a denominational label. The expression of belief and even the nature of belief may take new and unfamiliar forms.[1]

The following comments relate only to figures for the Church of England unless otherwise stated.

Infant baptisms Full tables for the years 1902–62 are given in Facts and Figures about the Church of England No. 3 (Tables 65–67 and diagram XII). The latest figure available from the Church Statistical Unit is for 1966 (511 per thousand live births).[2] This indicates that rather more than one child in two is brought forward for infant baptism. These figures exclude adult baptisms, and baptisms carried out in extra-parochial places of worship unless also registered in a parish register. Figures for parochial infant baptisms can, however, form a

---

[1]See, e.g. T. Luckmann, *The Invisible Religion*, Macmillan, 1967.
[2]*Church of England Yearbook*, 1970.

useful basis for comparison from diocese to diocese and from year to year; and in both respects, the average figures conceal marked variations. The figure for the provinces of Canterbury and York was 658 per thousand live births in 1902, and it rose steadily – for reasons which have never been explained – to a peak of 717 in 1928. Thereafter it began slowly to decline to the present level of 511,[1] though individual years, such as 1950 (672) have denied the trend. Differences between dioceses are considerable. In 1964, the four highest figures were those for Hereford (739), Worcester (695), Lincoln (682) and Norwich (682). The four lowest were London (346), Southwark (407), Liverpool (452) and Bradford (458). The rural/urban differential is fairly clearly established, but the causes are obscure. Fr Pierre Boulard, observing a similar differential in Easter Day communicants in France, concluded that rural areas were more traditional, and therefore more religious.[2] Leslie Paul, commenting on the baptism figures given here, saw a possible connection with the deployment of the clergy.[3]

26 *Confirmations* According to the Church Statistical Unit the Church had 9,957,000 confirmed members in 1966.[4] Population movement precluded the calculation of precise totals by dioceses, and the estimate (to the nearest thousand) is achieved by applying the confirmation rates for various years to the relevant age groups of the population as it existed in 1962. This is an established statistical method, but does not of course have the accuracy of direct recorded counts.
The record of actual confirmations year by year from 1911 to 1964 shows a drop in the confirmation rate from $42 \cdot 8$ per thousand young people aged 12–20 years to $25 \cdot 9$ per thousand in 1964.[5] The decline for boys (from $35 \cdot 8$ per thousand aged 12–20 to $20 \cdot 7$) is less than that for girls (from $49 \cdot 5$ to $31 \cdot 3$).

27 *Marriages* Marriage returns refer to England and Wales taken together – there are no separate tables for England. The inclusion of Wales, like the inclusion of Scotland in the Gallup Poll statistics, has the effect of decreasing the proportion of Anglicans. On this basis, the proportions per thousand marriages by type of solemnisation between 1904 and 1962, according to Facts and Figures, No. 3, Table 70, were as follows:

---

[1]The proportion of Roman Catholic baptisms has risen steadily in the same period.

[2]P. Boulard: *An Introduction to Religious Sociology*, trans. M. J. Jackson. Darton, Longman and Todd, 1960.

[3]L. Paul: *The Deployment and Payment of the Clergy*, Church Information Office, 1964, p. 23. 'The inevitable effect of the parochial system of employment is to place most of the parsons in the country while most of the population lives in the towns.'

[4]*Facts and Figures about the Church of England*, No. 3. Church Information Office, 1965, Table 71.

[5]*Facts and Figures about the Church of England*, No. 3, Table 68. If these figures sound very small in relation to the total of confirmed members, it should be remembered that young people stay in this age group for eight years, and their confirmation can take place in any one of those years.

	C of E and C in Wales	RC	Free Church	Jews	Civil Ceremonies
1904	642	41	131	7	179
1909	614	42	132	7	205
1914	583	47	122	7	241
1919	597	52	115	5	231
1924	578	55	122	7	238
1929	562	60	114	7	257
1934	535	65	109	7	284
1939 1944 1949	War years. No figures given				
1952	496	94	99	5	306
1957	496	115	104	5	280
1962	474	123	102	5	296

These figures show a decline in Anglican marriages and an increase in civil ceremonies in the first half of the century. There are signs that the popularity of civil marriage is now declining somewhat, but Anglican figures have continued to decrease. The outstanding factor in the last thirty years has been the increase of Roman Catholic marriages: it is difficult to determine how far this is due to the marriage discipline of the Roman Catholic Church, to differential birth-rates between Catholic and non-Catholic families in the earlier part of the century (resulting in larger numbers of Catholic young people coming forward for marriage) or to the effects of Catholic immigration. However, opinion polls do not suggest a significant rise in the proportion of the population claiming membership of the Roman Catholic Church.

If one excludes figures for the Churches in Wales, it is reasonable to say that about one marriage in two in the provinces of Canterbury and York takes place in an Anglican place of worship.

Parochial Easter communicants Facts and Figures about the Church of England, No. 3 gives a total number of parochial Easter communicants in 1922 as 2,317,000, or 89 per thousand of population aged 15 and over. There was a slight rise in the 1920s, and then a rather jerky drop to the 1962 figure of 2,347,000 or 69 per thousand. Up to 1962, the absolute numbers of Easter communicants increased, though they represented a smaller proportion of an expanding population. Since 1962, however, it appears that they have begun to drop in absolute terms. The figures for 1964 and 1966 are 2,141,750 and 2,074,673 respectively.

29   These figures include communicants in the week following Easter Day, but not Low Sunday, which is also within the octave.[1] Like baptism figures, they are based on parochial returns only and therefore exclude those attending Easter Communion in non-parochial establishments (including religious communities and retreat houses).

30   Easter Communion is often taken as the major indicator of the size and strength of Anglican Church membership. The 1662 Prayer Book rubric enjoins that 'every confirmed member of the Church shall communicate at the least three times a year, of which Easter to be one', but as we have already indicated in considering opinion polls, Easter communicants may not adequately represent the worshipping strength of the Church of England. In some areas, particularly in the North and Midlands, there is a strong tradition of Mattins-going in which Communion is seen as an occasional or even optional rite rather than as the central act of worship. One observer has suggested that a considerable number of regular churchgoers do not know of the existence of the ruling about Easter Communion.[2] Communicant figures need therefore to be interpreted with care. It is not sufficient to relate them to the whole population – 'two million out of 46 million': to be a communicant, a person has to be of a suitable age (which is why figures are computed in terms of the general population over the age of 15), confirmed and – to receive Communion in the parish church – physically mobile. Communicants in hospitals and residential homes are not included, and not all the housebound ask for or receive Communion at home, while those who do may not be included in the returns.

31   *Electoral roll enrolments* refer to the number of people who are entitled to attend the annual vestry meeting and to vote, or, if over 18, to stand as candidates in parochial church council elections. Since the annual parochial church meeting elects to the Deanery Synod, and the Deanery Synod to the Diocesan Synod and the General Synod, this is the basic group with a right to take part in church government. Persons on the electoral roll of a parish must be over the age of 17 years, and either resident in the parish or 'habitual attenders' at the parish church. Under the Synodical Government Measure, there are rules for the regular revision of electoral roll lists.

32   The number of persons enrolled has decreased very sharply, from 140 per thousand population of the appropriate age in 1924 to 81 in 1964.[3] These figures are based on returns made to diocesan secretaries in 1924, 1929, 1934, 1939, 1949, 1959, 1960 and 1964, and estimates by the Statistical Unit from returns made by incumbents in the inter-

---

[1]They would, however, involve multiple counting of persons receiving Communion more than once in Easter week.

[2]R. H. T. Thompson: *The Church's Understanding of Itself*. SCM Press, 1957.

[3]Facts and Figures about the Church of England, No. 3, Table 72.

vening years. The decline is certainly well-established, but is capable of more than one interpretation: it could mean a decline in involvement with the Church; a decline in participation in the organisational life of the Church (not necessarily correlated with a decline in belief or worship) or merely more efficient registration procedures which have removed from the rolls the names of people who have died, left the district, or ceased to attend church. In the first flush of enthusiasm for the scheme in the 1920s, the lists may well have been inflated.

LOCAL STUDIES

In the absence of the resources with which to carry out extensive nationwide surveys, some social scientists have opted for local, intensive studies. Clergy and parish groups, eager to have factual information about their local situation, have followed their example. These smaller studies often provide information about the variations in patterns of religious commitment which are masked by the national figures.

There are, however, considerable problems to be met in trying to piece together the information presented by such studies. There is little standardisation of method or of categorisation, so that the results of different surveys can seldom be usefully compared with one another.[1]

Existing survey material is of very uneven quality. Some of the most useful and reliable material comes from studies in which religious behaviour and practice is seen as one aspect of the total complex of social and economic life in a neighbourhood. Even these studies, which are organised and analysed by professional social scientists, are not often comparable with each other; but they do at least set the religious data against the local background needed for its interpretation. Surveys of this kind include the *Merseyside surveys*,[2] the *York surveys*,[3] the *Banbury survey*,[4] the *Institute of Community Studies surveys*,[5] the *Glossop survey*,[6] and the *Swansea survey*.[7] H. E. Bracey's *English Rural Life*[8] and W. M. Williams' *Gosforth: The Sociology of an English Village*[9] give similar data for rural areas. Recent local surveys support the opinion surveys

---

[1]An Account of 'Religion as a Key Variable' by Ernest Krausz, is shortly to be published by the Social Science Research Council and the British Sociological Association in their joint series on 'Comparability in Social Research'. This makes suggestions for the use of typologies.

[2]D. Caradog Jones: *Social Survey of Merseyside*, vol. 3, Liverpool UP, 1934.

[3]B. Seebohm Rowntree: *Poverty – A Study of Town Life* (1901). *Poverty and Progress* (1941) and *English Life and Leisure* (with B. R. Lavers) (1951).

[4]M. Stacey: *Tradition and Change*, OUP, 1960.

[5]P. Wilmott and M. Young: *Family and Kinship in East London*, Routledge, 1955; *Family and Class in a London Suburb*, Routledge, 1960; P. Townsend: *The Family Life of Old People*, and other studies.

[6]A. H. Birch: *Small Town Politics*, OUP, 1959.

[7]K. C. Rosser and C. C. Harris: *Family and Social Change*. Routledge, 1965.

[8]Routledge, 1959.

[9]Routledge, 1956.

in illustrating that large sections of the population wish to define themselves as 'Church of England'. This affiliation appears to occur in all regions of the provinces of Canterbury and York, irrespective of age, sex and social class. The following figures are abstracted from recent surveys:

CHURCH OF ENGLAND AFFILIATION – LOCAL SURVEYS

Area	Date	Coverage	% C. of E.
Banbury[1]	1959	all social classes	67·6
Banbury[2]	1968	all social classes	72·0
Hodge Hill, Birmingham[3]	1964	middle class area	58·0
Balsall Heath, Birmingham[4]	1963	working class area	60·0
Bishop's Stortford[5]	1965	commuter area	74·5
Hull[6]	1966	young married couples	61·0

35 These figures do not differ markedly from those reported by Leslie Paul for Roseworth, Stockton-on-Tees (1962 – 60·7 per cent); Morpeth (1962? – 67·2 per cent); and Sedgley, Worcs. (1962? – 65 per cent), and confirm the general findings of the Opinion Polls.

36 Some local surveys have produced figures for church attendance, based either on head-counts at services or on self-reported attendances. At first sight, these appear extremely low. The Rowntree studies of York (q.v.) suggested a decline in weekly attendance at Church of England services from 15·5 per cent of the adult population in 1901 to 7·46 per cent in 1935 and 4·3 per cent in 1948. Stockwood's survey at Bristol (1953) gave a figure of 4·9 per cent[7]; Colin Bell at Banbury (1968) got 1·92 per cent,[8] and P. Dodd at Rotherham (1965) 2 per cent[9]; but these figures need caution in interpretation, for several reasons. First, there are the indications from the opinion surveys that monthly attendance is now a better index of 'regular' Anglican

---

[1]M. Stacey: *Tradition and Social Change*, OUP, 1960.

[2]C. Bell: *New Society*, May 30th, 1968.

[3]C. R. Hinings: The Hodge Hill Survey, *Research Bulletin, University of Birmingham Institute for the Study of Religious Worship and Architecture*, 1967.

[4]C. R. Hinings: The Balsall Heath Survey, *Research Bulletin, University of Birmingham Institute for the Study of Religious Worship and Architecture*, 1967.

[5]A. Spencer: A Religious Census of Bishop's Stortford, in *A Sociological Yearbook of Religion in Britain*, D. Martin (ed.) 1968.

[6]J. Peel: The Hull Family Survey: I – The Survey of Couples, 1966. *Journal of Biosocial Science*, 2 (1). January 1970.

[7]Quoted by Michael Argyle, *Religious Behaviour*, Routledge, 1958, p. 6.

[8]C. Bell: *New Society*, May 30th, 1968.

[9]P. Dodd: 'Who Goes to Church?' *New Society*, April 29th, 1965.

church-going than weekly attendance. Second, rates of attendance vary considerably in different types of areas. Many of the surveys have been undertaken in precisely those areas where there is greatest concern because the churches are not filled. Third, Anglican attendance is of course a variable proportion of all religious observance. 'Regionally, Catholics are concentrated in the north-west and the London area. They are very infrequent in country districts and the south-west. Nonconformists are strong in the north-east and parts of the south-west (especially Cornwall). The Church of England appears strongest in Norfolk, Lincolnshire and the West Midlands . . .[1] If these factors are allowed for, there is not necessarily incongruity between the figures of the local surveys and those of national opinion surveys.

7 Local studies can examine in depth patterns of lapsing membership. It is reported in the studies of Rotherham and Scunthorpe[2] that only 30 per cent of those regularly attending church have done so all their lives. The age-structure of congregations suggests that there is a typical age-cycle in which people give up churchgoing in their teens and early twenties, but rejoin in their thirties and forties.

8 There appear to have been no attempts so far to use the techniques of the longitudinal survey to study this cyclical pattern of membership. Studies of lapsing among Methodists, however, suggest that one of the major factors is a change of job or a move to a new area. In such cases, lapsing is not a positive decision not to attend, but rather a failure to attend due to lack of social support and the pressures of making a new life.[3] This suggestion helps to explain the discrepancies between the objective counts of attendance, and the subjective claims of church affiliation. It also helps to explain the 'guilt' feelings reported of persons who do not attend church, but who think of themselves as church members.[4]

9 If further research confirms this interpretation, it will shed new light on the large group of 'nominal Anglicans'. It may be that they are not all merely people who like to call themselves 'C. of E.', and that a more accurate description of some would be 'intermittent Anglicans', since they are active members of the Church at some stages of their lives, but not at others.

SUMMARY OF STATISTICAL MATERIAL
(statistics for the provinces of Canterbury and York)

10 1. Nominal support for the Church of England, as estimated by public opinion surveys, is given by at least half and probably nearer two-

---

[1]David Martin: *A Sociology of English Religion*, SCM Press, 1967, p. 47.
[2]W. S. F. Pickering: Religious Movement of Church Members in Two Working Class Towns in England, *Archives de Sociologie de Religion* II, 1961.
[3]J. Butler, A Sociological Study of Lapsed Membership. *London and Holborn Review*, July 1966.
[4]M. Stacey, *op. cit.*, p. 71.

thirds of the adult population. Assuming that children under sixteen follow their parents' affiliation, this means that at least 23 million and probably over 30 million people regard themselves as 'C. of E.'.

2. More than one in four of the adult population have been confirmed – a total of nearly 10 million people.

3. One child in two is baptised in the Church of England.

4. One couple in two (or nearly so) is married in the Church of England.

5. According to opinion surveys, there are something like $4\frac{1}{2}$ million Roman Catholics in the two provinces, and nearly six million Free Churchmen.

6. The gap between affiliation statistics and attendance statistics is much larger for the Church of England than for other Churches in England. Only a small proportion, now slightly less than two million people per year, make their Easter Communion; however, there are some doubts as to whether this is an adequate index of membership, since attendance figures from local surveys suggest a much larger attendance on a once-monthly or several-times-a-year basis.

7. In terms of affiliation claims, the membership of the Church of England shows no bias of sex or age or social class; but regular church-goers tend to include larger numbers of women, older people and the upper socio-economic classes.

A NOTE ON SECONDARY MATERIAL

41 Information on religious behaviour and practice is of very uneven quality, and there is a need for major research projects to be mounted if our understanding of these very complex questions is to be deepened. In the last decade, social scientists in Britain and the United States have been increasingly drawn to the study of statistical material of the kind quoted here. As we have indicated, the material is fragmentary, confused and sometimes contradictory. It is not surprising that there have been conflicting interpretations.

42 A major debate has centred around the nature and meaning of the term 'secularisation'. Dr Bryan Wilson[1] has argued that 'Religious thinking, religious practices and religious institutions were once at the very centre of the life of western societies, as indeed of all societies . . . men act less and less in response to religious motivation'. In a complex urban society, areas of life will become both highly specialised and compartmentalised: thus we tend to make legal judgements about matters of law, economic judgements about economic issues, and medical

---

[1]*Religion in Secular Society*, New Thinkers' Library, Watts, 1966. Much of Wilson's thinking is based on the sociological concept of a shift from *Gemeinschaft*, or a small-scale, personal way of life, to *Gesellschaft* – the condition of mass society. See F. Tonnies: *Community and Association*, Routledge, 1955

judgements about disease, rather than making purely theological judgements about all three. This process is paralleled by the development of secular institutions: State schools have grown in numbers, and church schools have declined; local leadership is often expressed through political and recreational associations rather than church groups.

3 However, a number of writers have taken the view that the changes which are taking place do not imply that men are less religious: they imply the expression of religious faith in different ways from those accepted by previous generations. Dr David Martin[1] has stressed the fact that much of modern life is oriented towards the home, and not to communal activities taking place outside the home. 'Modern man is either mobile in his car or immobile in front of his television set'. Dr Milton Yinger[2] has argued that the development of religious toleration inevitably and necessarily implies the weakening of denominational attachment. Members of different Churches must share common non-denominational codes of behaviour if religion-based conflict is to be avoided. Robert Bellah takes the argument further by suggesting a new, non-denominational synthesis which he calls 'Civic Religion'.[3] Though Bellah is writing with reference to the United States, the application of this view with reference to the Church of England is hard to resist. It could be argued that much of the nominal support for the 'C. of E.' may be of this kind. However, Berger and Luckman point out that, as society becomes increasingly pluralistic, the State must increasingly withdraw from direct involvement in religious institutions.[4]

4 Professor E. K. Nottingham, also writing from the United States, argues that Church organisations face an inescapable dilemma. They must be effective in disciplining their members, in upholding the ideals and beliefs for which they were founded; and 'religious discipline, when accepted in its entirety, is exceedingly demanding'; at the same time, they must reach out to new members and strive to retain existing ones, even at the cost of compromise. This introductory text, which is anthropologically based, throws a good deal of light on the contradictory features of Anglican membership statistics.[5]

5 In recent years, the organisation of the Church of England has come under direct study. David Morgan studied the social background of

---

[1]D. Martin: 'The Secularisation Pattern in England', in *The Religious and the Secular*, SCM Press, 1969.

[2]J. M. Yinger: Pluralism, Religion and Secularisation, *Journal for the Scientific Study of Religion*, 6 (1) 1967.

[3]R. Bellah: Civic Religion in America, *Daedalus*, 1966.

[4]P. Berger and T. Luckmann: Secularisation and Pluralism, *Internationales Jahrbuch für Religionssoziologie, Theoretische Aspekte der Religionssozologie* (1) 1966.

[5]E. K. Nottingham: *Religion and Society*, Random House Studies in Sociology, New York, 1954.

English diocesan bishops.[1] A. P. M. Coxon has completed a thesis on the recruitment, selection and professional socialisation of Anglican ordinands,[2] while Robert Towler has analysed the reaction of the clergy to an increasingly specialised society.[3] P. F. Rudge has essayed a description of church administration in terms of different schools of organisation theory,[4] and K. A. Thompson has studied the way in which the organisation of the Church of England has adapted in relation to the changing structures of society.[5]

G. Bedouelle, writing from a Roman Catholic religious community near Paris, has produced a remarkable account of the Church of England against the background of contemporary society. While stressing the many paradoxical features in the life of the Church, and finding it 'often less Anglican than English', he rejects the view that England is now a secular society, and the explanation, advanced by some social historians, that this is a consequence of the estrangement of the working classes. He sees England as 'implicitly' Christian, with the Anglican tradition interwoven in the thinking of both the political right and the political left. 'On the basis of the Christian faith, the Church of England offers the society in which she lives her passion for liberty and her respect for individuals'.[6]

---

[1]Unpublished M.A. thesis (University of Hull), quoted in L. Paul: *The Deployment and Payment of the Clergy*, pp. 282–285.

[2]Ph.D. thesis (University of Leeds) 1965. Preliminary work was briefly reported in the Paul Report. See also 'An Elite in the Making', *New Society*, November 26th, 1964.

[3]R. Towler: The Changing Role of the Clergy, *Downside Symposium*, 1969, and Puritan and anti-Puritan: types of vocation to the ordained ministry. *A Sociological Yearbook of Religion in Britain*, 2. ed. D. Martin, SCM Press, 1969.

[4]P. F. Rudge: *Ministry and Management, the Study of Ecclesiastical Administration*. Tavistock Publications, 1968.

[5]K. A. Thompson: *The Organisational Response of the Church of England to Social Change, with special reference to the emergence of Church Assembly*. D.Phil. thesis (University of Oxford), 1968.

[6]G. Bedouelle: *L'Eglise d'Angleterre et la Société Politique Contemporaine*. Pichon and Durand-Azias, Paris, 1968.

APPENDIX E

The Church of Scotland

RELATION TO THE STATE

The constitution of the Church has been ratified and confirmed, rather than conferred, by the State, and all Statutes, Acts, Canons, etc. inconsistent with the constitution and powers conferred and recognised by the Act of 1592 have been repealed by it. Adhering to the substance of the faith of the Reformed Churches, and the presbyterian form of church government, the Church has a right to:

(1) frame its subordinate standards;
(2) constitute its own courts;
(3) legislate and judge in all matters of doctrine, government, worship and discipline, membership and office:
(4) appoint its agents and their spheres of service;
(5) alter its own constitution within prescribed limits and in accordance with prescribed procedure.

The authority and power of the Courts of the Realm is fully recognised in matters of property and civil right.

PATRONAGE

2 The patronage system was reformed by the Church Patronage Act of 1874, which, after reciting that the Crown had been graciously pleased to signify that it had placed at the disposal of Parliament its interest in the several rights of advocation, donation, and patronage, of churches and parishes in Scotland, (i) declared all rights of appointment to be vested in the congregations of vacant churches and parishes, subject to Regulations of General Assembly, and (ii) provided for the compensation of private patrons on application to the sheriff within six months after the passing of the Act, failing which all claims to compensation were to be taken as renounced. The amount of compensation was to be 'the average of the three preceding years' stipend from the teinds' (tithes), to be paid in four yearly instalments out of the stipend payable to the minister. (Compensation amounted therefore to one year's purchase of the benefice).

CHURCH FRANCHISE

3 The definition of the congregation was left to the General Assembly, which accordingly made regulations for the compiling of the roll of the congregation in each parish, such roll to consist of the names of:

(1) **All** communicants for the time being;

(2) **Adherents**, i.e. parishioners or seatholders of full age who have formally claimed in writing to be on the electoral roll, and in regard to whom the kirk session is satisfied that they desire to be permanently connected with the congregation or are associated with it in its interests and work, and that no reason exists for refusing to admit them to the Communion if they apply.

CONSTITUTION

4 The Scottish system of church government is based on the co-ordinate authority of the teaching elders (ministers ordained by the presbytery) and ruling elders (laymen set apart for the office by the minister). In all the assemblies of the Church the two sit and vote as one body – i.e. there is no 'vote by orders'. All elders (of both kinds) must at the time of their 'ordination' (the word is used for the setting apart of the ruling elder as well as for the ordination of the teaching elder) assent to the Confession of Faith and to the discipline, worship, and government of the Church as established by law.

(i) *Kirk Session* – Every parish has a kirk session. The minister is *ex officio* 'moderator'. There is no limit to the number of elders, who are selected by kirk session, and 'ordained' after adequate opportunity has been given for any objection to be raised. There must be at least two present in session with the minister to constitute a quorum.

5 The minister conducts public worship, administers the sacraments, and ordains and admits elders. He summons meetings, and has a casting vote in case of equality of voting. The kirk session assists him and in particular arranges the hours of service, judges of the fitness of applicants for church membership, exercises discipline, and grants to members certificates of fitness on removal from the parish. It keeps the roll of communicants (which it submits annually to the presbytery with the record of its proceedings), the roll of the congregation, the baptismal and banns registers. It sees that the Acts of Assembly are put into operation, and that collections are duly made.

6 In the case of the old parish churches the charges of maintenance of the fabric of the church and manse are borne by the 'heritors'; that is, roughly speaking, the landowners of the parish. In newly constituted parishes – *Quoad sacra* parishes, as they are called – they are borne by the congregation.

(ii) *Presbyteries* – These consist of an equal number of ministers and elders. Equality is achieved by providing for election by the kirk sessions within the district of a sufficient number of elders to equal the number of qualified ministers.

The moderator is elected and is by custom always a minister, all the ministers usually holding the office in rotation.

7   The presbytery regulates and controls the appointment and work of the ministers and deals with any charges or complaints against them. It can suspend or depose them. It tries presentees and conducts their ordination and induction, and grants licences to preach. Every minister on ordination promises to submit to the jurisdiction of the presbytery. Parishioners may present charges against him, and the presbytery may initiate proceedings in the case of *fama clamosa*. The presbytery can review *mero motu* all decisions of kirk sessions within its area.

8   The presbytery also determines all matters connected with glebes, and the erection and repair of churches and manses (subject to appeal to the civil court), and generally superintends the work of the parishes within its bounds.

9   Judgements may be enforced, if need be, by application to the civil courts, which alone have power to add civil consequences to ecclesiastical judgements.

(iii) *The Provincial Synod* – The presbyteries are grouped into provincial synods, each being composed of not less than three presbyteries. All members of the presbyteries included in the Synod are members of the synod. The synod meets twice a year, chiefly to deal with appeals and complaints from the presbyteries. It can also review *mero motu* the decisions of the presbyteries.

(iv) *The General Assembly* – The General Assembly is the supreme court of the Church in matters spiritual. Its decisions are final and are not subject to review by any civil court. The membership consists of commissioners elected by presbyteries for each assembly. These commissioners being ministers (including theological professors) and ruling elders, are elected in proportion to the size of each presbytery, one minister for every four or part of four ministers on the roll of the presbytery and an equal number of ruling elders. Ministers must be members of the presbyteries by which they are elected and elders must be *bona fide* acting elders of kirk sessions. Elections take place during the two months immediately preceding the month in which the General Assembly is to meet.

10 The General Assembly is presided over by a moderator elected immediately after it has been constituted. The moderator is nominated by a committee appointed by the outgoing General Assembly. The outgoing moderator constitutes the next Assembly and presides over it until his successor is elected.

11 *Method of Convention* – The General Assembly is not convened by the Crown, and may meet on its own initiative (Act of 1592). It is usual for each Assembly to fix the time and place of meeting for its successor, which is then notified by the moderator, and 'declared and intimated'

by the Lord High Commissioner, who attends the Assembly as representing the Sovereign, presents a royal letter, addresses the Assembly, and dissolves it after the moderator has dismissed it in the name of Christ. The Lord High Commissioner is not a member of the Assembly, and exercises no control over its business.

12 *Powers* –

    (1) The Assembly possesses full powers of legislation and administration. It can within prescribed limits alter its constitution. By the Barrier Act (an Act of Assembly passed in 1697) 'any Acts that are to be binding rules and constitutions of the Church' must, after passing through the General Assembly, be remitted for the consideration of the presbyteries, and require the approval of a majority of these. In 1736 the rule was applied to 'Acts rescissory of any standing Acts', and in 1848 to 'any Act which involves an essential alteration of the existing law or practice'. The Assembly may, however, pass interim Acts, which are valid till the next Assembly, and may (as the sole interpreter of its own laws) pass declaratory Acts.

    (2) The Assembly deals finally with complaints and appeals, and petitions against decisions of presbyteries. It may also review *mero motu* decisions of lower courts.

    (3) The Assembly also deals with 'overtures' (proposals for change in the law, practice, policy, etc., of the Church), appoints committees and deals with their reports, and alters the bounds of presbyteries. It has no power to create new parishes. It also appoints a 'Committee of Assembly' to act in the interval before the next Assembly meets, with specified powers.

INTERFERENCE BY CIVIL COURTS

13 Civil courts cannot interfere with anything done within the sphere of jurisdiction of the ecclesiastical courts, which are recognised judicatures of the realm. In no case will the civil court entertain an appeal from a judgement of an ecclesiastical court on a question of doctrine, or enter on an examination of the soundness of such judgement before enforcing its civil consequences. All matters of ritual are exclusively within the sphere of the ecclesiastical courts, but it is conceivable (though extremely improbable) that a case might arise in which flagrant departure from the form and purity of worship established by the Act of 1707, if uncorrected by the ecclesiastical courts, would justify an appeal to the civil courts. No appeal lies to a civil court in matters of discipline, or on the ground of excess of punishment, unless there is excess of jurisdiction (e.g. unless punishment is inflicted for obeying the law of the land).

14 On the other hand, the civil power is bound to 'give all due assistance for making the sentences and censures of the Church and her judicatures to be obeyed or otherwise effectual as accords' (Act of 1693).

The Presbyterian form of church government, and the Confession of Faith, are approved by the State, and the State would therefore have the right to be consulted on any proposal for changing these.

The civil courts hear and determine appeals on matters connected with church property, glebe, repair of churches, etc.

For nearly 300 years following the Reformation bitter controversy raged in the Church over the question of lay patronage. The right of the heritors (land-owning gentry) and elders to nominate a candidate to the presbytery for appointment to a vacant benefice was abolished in 1690 but restored by Queen Anne in 1712. The Act of 1712 attempted to preserve the right of the congregation to object to a presentee but in practice such objections appear to have been largely ignored by the presbyteries. In 1834 the General Assembly took steps to restore to the parishes an effective voice with the result that a presentation by the Earl of Kinnoul was refused and the presentee took the matter to the Court of Session, which found in his favour as did the House of Lords. Other cases followed.

The Church was split. The moderates held that the law must be obeyed and constitutional means adopted to get it amended. The evangelicals maintained that the Headship of Christ was threatened and that the action of the civil courts was obstructing the Church in the performance of its divinely appointed task. In 1843 the Evangelicals left the Church and formed the Free Church of Scotland. About one-third of the ministers and members of the Church went out.

Two other secessions had taken place earlier also on the issue of patronage and the Moderate policy of the General Assembly. The majority of these united in 1847, to form the United Presbyterian Church and in 1900 that body joined the Free Church of Scotland to form the United Free Church. A small group of Free Churchmen, mostly in the Highlands, refused to enter the union of 1900 and successfully claimed to be the Free Church and thus entitled to its property. They took their case to law and won. Legislation was necessary to put matters straight.

The successful accomplishment of one union turned men's minds to the possibilities of another, and a joint commission was set up by the Church of Scotland and the United Presbyterian Church in 1909, the result of whose labours were the Church of Scotland Act, 1921, and the Declaratory Articles appended to it. It should be noted that the Act does not enact the Declaratory Articles but declares them to be lawful.

APPENDIX F

Evidence Received

Those who gave oral evidence are marked with *. Those who gave both written and oral evidence are marked with a †, while those who gave written evidence only are unmarked.

Abdy, Mr C. L.
Alison, Mr M., MP
Arbuthnot, Sir John, Bt, MBE, TD, a Church Commissioner
Barry, the Rt Rev. F. R. (lately Bishop of Southwell)
Beaumont of Whitley, the Rev. the Lord
*Beloe, Mr R. L., CBE, then Lay Secretary to the Archbishop of Canterbury
British Humanist Association, the
*Baptist Union of Great Britain and Ireland, the (the Rev. Dr D. S. Russell, the Rev. H. L. Watson and Mr J. G. Le Quesne, QC)
*Butler, the Rt Rev. B. C., (Auxiliary Bishop of Westminster)
*Canterbury, the Archbishop of, (the Most Rev. and Rt Hon. Dr A. M. Ramsey)
Central Churches Group of the National Council of Social Service
C.H.U.R.C.H., a Christian Anarchist group of
Church Assembly Board for Social Responsibility, the
†Church Commissioners, the (the Lord Silsoe, GBE, MC, TD, QC, Sir H. Ashton, KBE, MC, DL, and Sir R. Harris, KCVO, CB)
†Church Society, the (the Rev. G. Marchant)
Church Union, the
Church of England Evangelical Council, the
†Church of England Youth Council, the (the Rev. R. Herbert)
*Congregational Church in England and Wales, the (the Rev. J. Huxtable and Sir Harold Banwell)
Denniston, Mr R.
Dickinson, the Rev. G.
Doble, Cdr D., a member of the House of Laity
*Episcopal Church of Scotland, the Primus of (the Most Rev. Dr F. H. Moncreiff)
Esdaile, the Rev. A. G. K., Vicar of All Saints, Mitcham
†Grubb, Sir K., KCMG, LLD, (then Chairman of the House of Laity of the Church Assembly)
Hardy, the Rev. D. P., Rector of Coton, Cambridgeshire
Hennell, the Rev. M. M., Principal of Ridley Hall
*Hogg, the Rt Hon. Quintin, QC, MP (now Lord Hailsham)

Howard, the Rev. S. R. K., Vicar of St Paul's, Cheltenham

Huron, the Bishop of (the Rt Rev. Dr G. N. Luxton)

Jackson, the Rev. M. J. (lately Sheffield Industrial Mission)

James, the Rev. Canon E. A. (Precentor Southwark Cathedral)

Jenkins, the Rev. Canon D. E., (then Fellow of the Queen's College, Oxford)

Johnston, Mr O. R., (then a member of the House of Laity)

Kimpton, Mr A. C. W., a member of the House of Laity, a Church Commissioner

*Lampe, the Rev. Professor G. W., Ely Professor of Divinity, Cambridge

†Latimer House (the Rev. Dr J. I. Packer)

Lloyd, Miss G. M.

McKenna, Miss M. R.

*Methodist Church (the Rev. Dr E. W. Baker, Secretary of the Methodist Conference, and the Rev. W. N. C. Wooldridge)

Missionary and Ecumenical Council of the Church Assembly, the

Moore, Chancellor the Rev. E. Garth

Modern Churchmen's Union, the

*Moule, the Rev. Professor C. F. D., Lady Margaret's, Professor of Divinity, Cambridge

Maltby and Bramley parishes discussion group (the Rev. C. Auckland)

National Council for Civil Liberties, the

National Secular Society, the

*Nineham, the Rev. D. E., (then Regius Professor of Divinity, Cambridge)

Partridge, the Rev. A., All Saints, Sydenham

Paul, Mr Leslie

*Payne, the Rev. Dr E. A., CH

†Presbyterian Church of England (the Rev. A. L. Macarthur, the Rev. J. C. O'Neill, the Rev. H. M. Springbett and Mr J. M. Ross, CBE)

*Reith, the Rt Hon. the Lord, KT, GCVO, GBE, CB, TD (lately Lord High Commissioner to the General Assembly of the Church of Scotland)

*Robinson, the Rt Rev. Dr J. A. T. (then Bishop of Woolwich)

*Rupert's Land, the Archbishop of (the Most Rev. Dr H. H. Clark, Primate of the Anglican Church of Canada)

Saumarez Smith, Mr W. H.

Scutcheon, Mr G.

Shackleton, Mrs T.

*Short, the Rt Hon. E. W., MP

†Stepney, the Bishop of (the Rt Rev. Dr E. U. T. Huddleston)

*Strong, the Most Rev. Dr P. N. W., KCMG (then Archbishop of Brisbane)

Taunton, the Bishop of (the Rt Rev F H West)

*Wales, the Archbishop of (the Most Rev. Dr W. G. H. Simon)

Wand, the Rt Rev. Dr J. W. C. (lately Bishop of London)

Wansey, the Rev. J. C., Vicar of Roydon

Warr, the Very Rev. Dr C. L., GCVO (Dean of the Chapel Royal in Scotland)

Wigglesworth, Chancellor W. S., DCL

William Temple Association, the, a study group of

†Williams, Sir G. G., KBE, CB, Secretary of the Churches Main Committee

*Willink, the Rt Hon. Sir H., Bt, MC, QC, DCL (Dean of the Arches)

West Lewisham Sub-deanery Chapter (the Rev. H. L. Katin)

*York, the Archbishop of (the Most Rev. and Rt Hon. Dr F. D. Coggan)

†York University, Department of Sociology (Mr R W Coles and Dr C Campbell)

APPENDIX G

Consultants from Other Churches

Mr J. G. Le Quesne, QC, Baptist Union
The Rev. J. Huxtable, Congregational Church
The Rev. Dr Eric Baker and The Rev. W. N. C. Wooldridge, Methodist
    Church
Mr J. M. Ross, CBE, Presbyterian Church of England
The Rt Rev. B. C. Butler, Roman Catholic Church

5789-1
124